Life and Chimes

A UNIQUE ACCOUNT OF PORTSMOUTH'S CHAMPIONSHIP YEAR 2002-03

Richard Holledge

Based on his column in The Times

Published by First Stone
A Division of Corpus Publishing Limited
4/5 The Marina, Harbour Road, Lydney,
Gloucestershire GL15 5ET

Photographs: Dave Jordan
Cover design: Lance Bellers

Printed by Bell & Bain Ltd., Glasgow

10 9 8 7 6 5 4 3 2 1

CONTENTS

ACKNOWLEDGEMENTS

All photography by **Dave Jordan**

The author would like to express his thanks to:
Yakubu Aiyegbeni, Rory Allen, Alan Ball, Karen Barnett, Basher
Benfield, Keith Blackmore, The Blue Bazookas, Kevin Bond, Mark
Burchill, Deon Burton, Kevin Cameron of Concurrent Design, Tracey
Campion, Carolyn Cavele, Steve Carthew-Butcher, Jason Crowe,
Debbie on the front desk, Arjan De Zeeuw, Lassina Diabate, Andy
Dobbs, Heather Emery of Classique Lingerie, Gianluca Festa, Hayden
Foxe, Andy Gardner, Des Gauntlett, Elaine Giles, Mike Hancock MP,
Vince Hilaire, Shaka Hislop, Eddie Howe, Richard Hughes, Tim
Hallissey, Kevin Harper, Barry Harris, Ray Hiron, Yoshi Kawaguchi,
Jamie Kennea and the Pompey Anoraks, Mick Kennedy, the landlord at
the Drum and Monkey, Ipswich, Mark Libby of Capileo tattooists,
Milan Mandaric, James McIntosh, Sam Matterface, Paul Merson,
Giuseppe Mascia of Pizza House, Neil Monnery, Johnny Moore,
Mike Newman, Vincent Pericard, Nigel Quashie, Gary O'Neil, Richard
Owen, Steve Pearson, John Phillips, Linvoy Primus, Janice Prior, Mick
Quinn, Tim Rice, Robertson, Carl Robinson, Kevin Ryan, Tim
Sherwood, Imogen Shrimpton, Tara Snowden, Jason Stone, Ben
Stoneham, Steve Stone, Mark Storey, Peter Storrie, Matthew Taylor,
Efsathios Tavlaridis, Carl Tiler, Marlene and Paddy Thomas, Svetoslav
Todorov, Nigel Tresidder, Sergeant Fiona Voller, John PFC Westwood,
And **Harry 'n' Jim.**

I have spent much of the season laughing at my friend, Richard Holledge. Not productive, I know, but I can't help it. Richard writes a weekly column for this paper about his beloved Portsmouth. It was supposed to be one of those gloomy diaries in which he would reflect with melancholy on his lot in life, but it has all gone badly wrong. Portsmouth are storming towards the Barclaycard Premiership and Richard has been reduced to writing about how well things are going. It's good stuff but offends every journalistic instinct.
Danny Finkelstein, who writes a column on betting for *The Times*.

A quote from Sky News during the Iraq conflict.
"Umm Qasr is a city similar to Southampton," UK defence minister Geoff Hoon said in The Commons yesterday.

"He's either never been to Southampton, or he's never been to Umm Qasr," says a British Squaddie patrolling Umm Qasr. Another soldier added: "There's no beer, no prostitutes and people are shooting at us. It's more like Portsmouth."

Portsmouth Football Club, however, remind me of a seaside resort having fallen on hard times, suffering from a prolonged spell of bad weather. Despairing landladies with vacancies in the windows of their bed and breakfasts, old men sheltering beneath umbrellas on deserted beaches and under-empoyed ice cream salesmen waiting for the sun.
Sergio Burns, *True Blue*, the supporters' magazine.

INTRODUCTION

It could have been Brighton. It was almost Spurs – well, their Sixties side was the most glorious of the last century – but, because of my best mate at school, it became Portsmouth. He said he supported them, so I did too. Simple as that. He hadn't explained that they were the worst team in the old First Division at the time, and later owned up to supporting Crystal Palace. But by then, despite the fact that they stumbled from crisis to crisis and I had never even seen them play, I was hooked. Portsmouth 'til I die.

I studiously kept scrapbooks about Freddie Cox's latest brilliant wheezes, tales of grim relegation battles in far-away Lincoln or Huddersfield, occasional shock wins like the one in the League Cup against Chelsea, and the first time we won the championship in the old Third Division. It was a helpless addiction, confirmed when I went to my first game with the best mate (Portsmouth 2 Rotherham 0). We were quite delirious with excitement. Our cheers echoed round the peace of the South Stand, to the profound irritation of the old boys around us, one of whom, finally driven crazy by our treble pipings, told us to be quiet. Or words to that effect.

Just as there is a time in our lives that is defined by pop records – *God Only Knows* by The Beach Boys, *Keep On Running* by Spencer Davis, *Terry* by Twinkle, *Ride Your Pony* by every college band at every dance I ever went to – so every supporter has a side he will never forget. Mine was the team of the late Sixties, and I used to share my admiration for them with a girl from Southsea with pink lips and a disapproving father. I used to drag her along to the home games until she went off with a bloke who owned a Lambretta. I don't think he supported Pompey either.

The serious love affair continued. What an outfit: Bobby Kellard, George Smith, Albert McCann, George Ley, Nicky Jennings and John McClelland. Oh, and dogged Ray Pointer up front. We watched that great nearly-side from the North Stand just behind the Mike Trebilcock Appreciation Society.

Once you've started to support a team, you can't change, however much they let you down. I used to see them in out-of-the-way places such as Oldham, Rochdale and Bury. I never saw them win, nor even draw. It's worse if you are an out-of-towner like me. It's hard to explain why, after the four-hour journey to the south coast and back, that 'no', you didn't have a good time, and 'yes', they did lose again. So why did I keep going? Because I was waiting for a season like the one we have just had, and, amazingly, I was given the opportunity of sharing the addiction with readers of *The Times*. We expected it to be yet more in the saga of despair: it was, of course, the finest season for 50 years.

"Top of the League," we chanted, "Harry is our King". But the song that does it for me, just as it did in that Rotherham game 40-odd years ago, is the *Pompey Chimes*, the great tribal chant that has united the supporters through the years of thin and thin. Ah, yes, as I used to say to the girl from Southsea: "They're playing our tune."

CHAPTER 1

AUGUST

August 10

HOPE AND GLORY

Ah, the first game of the season. Sunshine, shirtsleeves, unbounded optimism. And it doesn't really matter if you lose. After all, there are 45 more games to get it right.

Even if your club has been put into administration, sold the best player, been digitally challenged and – in the ultimate gesture of despair – signed Gazza, for most fans this is the best day of the season. Play-offs? Promotion? Why not.

Take Portsmouth. Every season for the past half-dozen the Fratton faithful have come streaming back to belt out the Pompey Chimes in welcome to yet another new manager, another new team, then brace themselves for the same old, woeful, story. But when hope springs...

I once skipped an Isle of Wight festival (two years after the big one with Bob) because it clashed with the opening game of the season against Middlesbrough. They had this new manager, Geordie lad called Jack Charlton. They won the game 2-0 and the championship by a mile, and Pompey finished nowhere.

This season it's going to be different. There's a new manager, Harry Redknapp, the fifth in five seasons. His wheeler-dealing on the transfer market makes Arthur Daley look like the Archbishop of Canterbury. He has managed to get shot of about 11 workaday players from a huge squad of 40-plus.

He has excited the fans by buying nine new players since he took over – or is it ten? There was talk of some Italian superstar yesterday. He has paraded a flurry of triallists, flying them in from obscure places, such as Ukraine and Belgium, to appear in friendlies against Havant or Newquay, only for them to disappear.

There were more rumours of close-season signings than changes to Manchester United's away kit: David Ginola, who was not worth it after all, Fabrizio Ravanelli, on a scheme that involved Pompey and Derby sharing his wage bill, Dion Dublin, Ronaldo (well, he ruled himself out by missing the Isle of Wight ferry and not making the friendly against Farnborough) and Paul Merson. That one turned out to be a runner. He has actually signed a two-year contract. Could be the best thing to happen to Portsmouth since Bobby Kellard.

Redknapp has bought shrewdly. He says. Thanks to the sale of Peter Crouch to Aston Villa for about £5 million, he has had money to spend on the likes of Richard Hughes and Eddie Howe from Bournemouth, Hayden Foxe, Shaka Hislop and Svetoslav Todorov from West Ham's seconds, and a French lad on loan from Juventus, who looks a bit sharp. He has picked up Matthew Taylor – a bargain, disgruntled Luton fans tell me – and Wigan Athletic superstar Arjan De Zeeuw. Oh, and yesterday he hired Deon Burton, the former Portsmouth forward, in case we were getting bored.

It's going to be tough on the fans today for the sell-out game against Nottingham Forest; they will hardly recognise a single player. It's reminiscent of the 1970s, which was a catastrophic time for the club (the Nineties and Noughties were merely nightmarish).

The manager, Ron Tindall, specialised in non-stop transfer activity. For four heady years he spent, spent, spent and the club slumped, slumped, slumped. One of the busiest years in the transfer market was 1972, the season of the club's 75th anniversary. It got everyone excited but the club finished 15th.

Of course, that can't happen 30 years on. Redknapp has made one bargain signing by making Jim "Bald Eagle" Smith his assistant manager. The 61-year-old Smith almost took the club to the FA Cup Final in 1992.

Redknapp has also been lucky. Two of the club's better strikers are almost back in action after long lay-offs. Poor Rory Allen has played only ten games in three years after seven operations on his knees, and Gary Burchill, who was injured after only a handful of games last season, played in some friendlies. He has inherited some good young players, such as Gary O'Neill, who have come via the youth team.

Play-offs? Promotion? Why not. We haven't heard that kind of talk since, well, last season, when Graham Rix was manager and Crouch was one of several new signings. Rix was sacked, Crouch was sold and the club scraped miserably clear of relegation.

But that was last year.

ANORAK'S CORNER

August 10
Portsmouth 2 Nottingham Forest 0
Scorers: Burton (8), Pericard (45)
Crowd: 18,910
Team: Hislop, Howe (Primus), Taylor, De Zeeuw, Foxe, Robinson, Quashie, O'Neil, Merson, Pericard, Burton.
Substitutes: Kawaguchi, Crowe, Barrett, Burchill.

Deon Burton came back to the club he left in 1997 and celebrated his second debut by scoring after eight minutes. New signing Vincent Pericard, on loan from Juventus, looked cool for a 19-year-old and scored with a diving header on half time. The midfield, Merson, Quashie and Robinson, were creative and Taylor was eager and effective on the left as Pompey dominated the second half. Eddie Howe – injured on his debut last season as one of Redknapp's first signings – dislocated his kneecap ten minutes after the start. Primus took over.

August 13
Sheffield United 1 Portsmouth 1
Scorer: Burton (25)
Crowd: 16,093
Team: Hislop, Primus, Taylor, De Zeeuw, Foxe, Robinson, Quashie (Hughes), O'Neil, Merson, Pericard (Todorov), Burton.
Substitutes: Kawaguchi, Crowe, Burchill.

Deon Burton scored the equalizer but should have bagged a hat trick in what was Pompey's third point ever at Bramall Lane in 22 games over an amazing 47 years.

August 17

THE FIGHT IS ON

Wow. What a start to the season. Within seconds of the train pulling into Cosham station, the first beer can of the season had been tossed at me. Minutes later, the fans piling out of Fratton Station were in a running fight with the Notts Forest contingent while the police joined in, administering a few whacks around the arms and legs with evil-looking steel truncheons.

Weird people these hooligans, all that 'you-looking-at-me?' posturing with unfit, pasty bodies and rippling tattoos. Every one terified they might actually get into a punch up.

Still, their ridiculous behaviour made sure we got to the ground late. Thanks lads.

The Fratton Faithful were barely in their seats when Deon Burton, back with the club after a ten-year break with Derby and Stoke, put Pompey ahead. He leapt so high in celebration, we thought he was going to end up in the Southsea. Vincent Pericard, who scored what Paul Merson rated a goal worthy of the Premiership, was the epitome of cool, barely raising his hands for a high five.

Harry 'It's a buyer's market' Redknapp was happy with his nine new signings and the fans were in ecstasy at half time, but it was an ecstasy tinged with reality.

'False' and 'dawn' are the two words that are frequently applied to Portsmouth FC.

It was only 12 months ago that Graham Rix was hailed as the Messiah and many fans are still shocked by the way he was sacked. Paddy Thomas, chairman of the supporters' club, was utterly disillusioned at the time and even now still feels 'pangs' at the way he was treated. Poor Rix was stabbed in the back so often, his enemies had run out of angles to get the knife in.

But Paddy does like the look of the new team, and salutes

Redknapp for his brilliant coup in signing Paul Merson.

What's more, so does fellow stalwart Basher Benfield, the most pessimistic supporter in Portsmouth, who stunned a social evening recently by declaring he thought this side could go all the way.

Paddy Thomas saw his first game when Pompey were champions. He and his dad took the ferry from Gosport and he was perched on the rails of the old North Stand. Pompey won the championship two years in succession in those fabulous Forties. Since then, he has supported the club through 50-plus years of thin and thin.

Another full-time fan, Neil Monnery, who runs the fans' website, is only 19 and has endured a mere dozen years of disappointment.

"The first game I watched was Charlton at home in 1990. We lost 1-0 and it was a terrible game, but I was hooked and now it's in my blood. You have to support your local side, don't you?"

He too was a big Rix fan.

"He was taking steady steps, building up the team slowly by bringing in young players. That's not Redknapp's style at all. He loves lots of activity and he wants instant results."

Both these keepers of the flame have an uneasy relationship with the club they support.

"We are independent of the club," says Paddy Thomas, "But sometimes we are in conflict with it and feel we have to criticise it, and they don't like criticism."

Or as Neil Monnery, whose Pompey fans' website attacked the sale of striker Peter Crouch last season, said: "I have to try to be fair but the things you hear about what goes on in the boardroom – it's like Mulder and Scully in the *X-Files*. You couldn't make it up."

And so to Palace today. Neil Monnery is still scarred (aren't we all?) by the terrible 4-2 defeat at their hands two seasons ago, which damn near condemned the club to relegation.

"It was awful, really awful, pissing down with rain, one of those days when you walk home wondering 'What am I doing here?'"

The first time I went there was a million years ago when Palace had money and were heading towards the old Division One. We stood on an earth mound that masqueraded as a stand. I think it's a supermarket now.

Many years later, Pompey had to win to stay in with a chance of promotion. Must have been in the mid-Eighties. The away supporters had kept up a barrage of triumphalist noise until the 89th minute when Palace's John Salako scored the winner with a minute to go.

The silence was deafening. But at least it wasn't raining.

ANORAK'S CORNER

August 17
Crystal Palace 2 Portsmouth 3
Scorers: Foxe (67) Crowe (69, 72)
Crowd: 18,315
Team: Hislop, Primus, Taylor, De Zeeuw, Foxe, Robinson (Crowe), Quashie, O'Neil, Merson, Pericard (Todorov), Burton.
Substitutes: Kawaguchi, Hughes, Burchill.

To the horror of the 4,000 away fans, Crystal Palace were winning 2-0 at half time and looked comfortably in control. Redknapp had a quiet word with his players at half time and substituted Crowe for Robinson and Todorov for Pericard, who then galvanized Pompey into a fightback. Foxe scored with a header in the 67th minute. Two minutes later, Taylor centred and Crowe side footed into the goal. Three more minutes, and after a neat move with Burton, he scored again. Hot day, hot stuff.

August 24

SURVIVE AND PROSPER

Half time and the place was like a morgue. Portsmouth 2-0 down to Crystal Palace and it was looking like the start to last season: played three, won one, drawn one, and about to lose one. So what's Harry Redknapp been up to? He's bought ten new players and we're back where we started. Terrible mistake selling Shaun Derry to Palace last week. It'll all start falling apart now...

Even two substitutions at half time and a tactical switch didn't make much difference. But then Paul Merson, who had looked knackered, rouses himself and lays on the pass that leads to Hayden Foxe scoring. And within four dizzying minutes, Jason Crowe has scored twice, Redknapp's a genius, it's bye-bye Palace and who's Shaun Derry anyway?

The guy who didn't get much of a write-up was midfielder Nigel Quashie, who covered every blade of grass, passed well, tackled soundly and kept his cool (important that, because he held the dubious honour of picking up 11 yellow cards last season).

Quashie is the only player in the first team from last year, along with Gary O'Neil, to have survived the Redknapp revolution. In the three years since he was bought for £200,000 from Forest, he has promised much but never quite shown the consistency that made Forest pay £2.5 million for him when he was a teenager. Fans at Queens Park Rangers, his previous club, told me he could be brilliant, but moody, and a touch defeatist.

Last season, the Pompey fans' website was admonitory: "Nigel Quashie needs to knuckle down and work on the basics. He has all the attributes of being a top-notch midfielder, he just needs to get it all together."

To judge from the first three games, he is getting it together.

Quashie, who is married with a daughter, one-year-old Ella, is philosophical. "A few years ago, my son was born prematurely and died, and that has put everything in perspective. When there is a new manager, you are bound to feel uncertain and wonder if you have a future. Every manager wants to bring in their new players and they have their own ideas, but something that I have learnt is that you just have to get on with life."

So impressive was his pre-season form that Redknapp offered him the club captaincy, which he held for two proud weeks until the arrival of Merson.

"I took the offer with both hands, but when Paul came to the club, I told Harry it would be better for the players if he was captain. It wasn't a hard decision to make, not at all, I just took it in my stride, I wasn't fussed."

Nor is he fussed by the influx of new talent. "It's like I'm a new player in a new team. The spirit is good and we are all determined to make the Premiership. It's what we're here for."

What about that moody jibe? "I am not a moody person. I just want to win, and if things aren't going well, I have my say."

He's also rather thoughtful. He had heard that Sunderland player Jody Craddock had lost a baby and said: "I'd like him to know that I feel for him. I know what he and his family are going through and they should know football is thinking of them."

Latest from 'Arry's Bargain Basement: The manager was linked with three new signings last week. Gianluca Festa, from Middlesbrough, Moreno Torricello, from Fiorentina, and Redknapp is in hot pursuit of Tottenham's Tim Sherwood. All free transfers, of course. As Harry put it: "There are deals to be done." He should know.

ANORAK'S CORNER

August 24

Portsmouth 3 Watford 0

Scorers: Merson (42), Todorov (45), Burton (47)

Crowd: 17,901

Team: Hislop, Crowe, Taylor, De Zeeuw, Foxe, Festa, Quashie, Hughes (Robinson), Merson (O'Neil), Todorov, Burton (Burchill).

Substitutes: Kawaguchi, Primus.

Paul Merson ran the show and scored a penalty in a convincing win. It was his cross that led to Todorov scoring on half time, and, 90 seconds into the second half, Burton's close shot put the game beyond doubt. This was Gianluca Festa's debut and he was impeccable (for this game and the rest of the season).

August 26

Grimsby 0 Portsmouth 1

Scorer: Burchill (82)

Crowd: 5,770

Team: Hislop, Crowe (Harper), Taylor, De Zeeuw, Foxe, Festa, Quashie, Hughes, Merson, Todorov (Robinson), Burton (Burchill).

Substitutes: Kawaguchi, Primus.

Portsmouth moved to the top of the Nationwide First Division after a difficult encounter watched by more than 1,000 Pompey fans. Substitute Mark Burchill scored with a fine left-foot drive.

August 31

A SONG IN MY HEART

Sometimes the excitement can be unbearable. Who would have thought that, with five matches gone, Portsmouth would be unveiling a new song to greet the team as they run on to the pitch? Who said that Harry Redknapp and his assistant manager, Jim Smith, were merely football maestros? These guys are movers and groovers, the Flanagan and Allen of the first division.

It turns out that they themselves chose the new song, *Let Me Entertain You*, by Robbie Williams. Younger readers – such as Harry, 54, and Jim, 61 – know the words:

Hell is gone and Heaven's here (we can only hope. Still, top after five matches is pretty heavenly).

There's nothing left for you to fear (but, they haven't played any of the division's better teams). Shake your arse, come over here (would have applied to the slow-moving, chain-smoking Robbie Prosinecki last season).

The idea is to rouse the crowd, as if they could be more ecstatic than they are with the best start to the season (played five, won four, drawn one) since 1948, back when, as many are amazed to discover, Pompey won the championship not once, but twice, in successive seasons.

The club had a similar start in 1922 in the old Third Division South, and won the first five matches in 1979-80 before being promoted from the old Fourth Division. Nothing like a statistic or two to bring a glow to the anoraks in the Fratton End.

Or, apparently, a good song. The club will also play the *Pompey Song* by local troubadour Shep Wooley – don't mock, he appeared at this year's Isle of Wight Festival with a Dylan tribute band. But anything is better than the unintentionally hilarious entrée for the past few seasons, Richard Strauss's *Thus*

Sprach Zarathustra (aka the theme to *2001, A Space Odyssey*), which provided an overture of gravity and folie de grandeur that contrasted somewhat with the farcical performances on the pitch and in the boardroom.

That had replaced Mike Oldfield's rather genteel little instrumental, *Portsmouth*, which was about as inspirational as a wet weekend in Southsea.

It reminds me of the first match of the 1965 season: new manager, George Smith; new team: a squad of only 16 players and a note in the programme by one Jimmy Dickinson welcoming the "wind of change" at the club, where "income would be balanced against expenditure". The music? *Hearts of Oak* and *Life on the Ocean Wave* performed by the Portsmouth City Fire Brigade Band.

The Arts Editor at *The Times*, a stranger to the feverish world of football but an enthusiast for the works of Mr Williams, rates Harry 'n' Jim's choice. "It was used by the alternative comedian, Lenny Beige, as part of his cabaret warm-up and Robbie sings it to get the crowds going. It has enormous energy, like The Rolling Stones' *Gimme Shelter*, with a great piano riff at the beginning."

Fact is, the home crowd are so fanatical that if it was uplifted much more it would float out to sea. The fans have one of the great club chants in the *Pompey Chimes*, which transcends even the complete lack of rhythm from a demented drummer and a tuneless bugler.

This column was going to be about Mark Burchill, the Scottish striker who played five games last season, scored four, then tore a cruciate ligament during a practice kickabout and missed the whole of the season. He came on against Grimsby on Monday, missed three sitters, scored a brilliant winner.

But I found Robbie Williams had got there first by singing: "He may be good, he may be outta sight."

'Arry's Bargain Basement continued. Redknapp missed out on signing Tim Sherwood from Spurs but got Gianluca Festa on a free and persuaded Middlesbrough to pay half the wages. That's 12 players in and 15 out since he took over and there's still today to go before the transfer deadline. Redknapp said: "I said I wanted a new team and that's what I've gone out and got."

ANORAK'S CORNER

August 31

Portsmouth 4 Brighton 2

Scorers: Taylor (3), Merson (26), Todorov (45), Crowe (52)

Crowd: 19,031

Team: Hislop, Crowe, Taylor, De Zeeuw, Foxe, Festa, Quashie, Hughes, Merson, Todorov, Burton.

Substitutes: Kawaguchi, Primus, Harper, Robinson, Burchill.

Six games, five wins. Mmmm. After three minutes, Merson chipped a delicate through-ball for wing-back Taylor to score, but Brighton hadn't read the script and not only equalized but went ahead. Luckily, Burton was judged to have been fouled in the penalty area and Merson glided the ball home. Todorov scored from a Taylor centre right on half time, and Crowe wrapped it up with a cracking shot into the top left-hand corner of the net. A 'lustrous performance' purred the reporter from The Times.

CHAPTER 2
SEPTEMBER

September 7
STARS IN OUR EYES

They don't do celebrity in Portsmouth. It's not the most fashionable place. OK, there's a new shopping centre on an old wharf with a Ralph Lauren outlet, Gap, Crew as well as a Paul Smith, and one or two players have made the national stage, such as Neil Webb, Mark Hateley, Mick Channon, but that was before or after their time at the club. For a true superstar, you'd have to go back to Jimmy Dickinson who played from the championship years of 1948 to a fight against relegation from the old Second Division in 1965.

The same goes for Pompey fans – they are distinctly low on the celebrity front.

No doubt Charles Dickens, who was born in the city, would have bought a season ticket and might even written a vignette for Harry 'n' Jim in the travelling theatre made unforgettable by Mr Vincent Crummles in *Nicholas Nickleby*.

Then there is the talented Mr Anthony Minghella, who won an Oscar for *The English Patient* and spends too much of his time away from Fratton Park, choosing instead to spend his (professional) time with the likes of Kristin Scott-Thomas and Gwyneth Paltrow and most recently Nicole Kidman, who stars in his next film, *Cold Mountain*. Mmm. Nicole Kidman in the Fratton End. Might put the drummer off his stroke.

Minghella was heroic a few years ago when the club faced administration, coming to public meetings, raising the browbeaten profile and helping to raise cash.

Brian Howe, lead singer from Bad Company, is another; he always seemed to be on the verge of buying the place in the Nineties, and Mick Jones of Foreigner seemed to have a sense of what was to come with his (hopefully) presciently-titled *I Have Waited So Long*.

And then there is Mick Robertson, who presented the children's show *Magpie* in the Seventies. You know, it was the one created to compete with *Blue Peter* and had Jenny Hanley as the sexy one – in a wholesome sort of way – to appeal to the dads. Robertson was the one with Marc Bolan hair – or Gilbert O'Sullivan depending how unkind you feel – and a big smile, and he is a fanatical Pompey man.

Now managing director of Wised Up, a TV company that specialises in children's programmes, he told me: "If I don't see a game, I get withdrawal symptoms. I have to wrestle with myself if I can't get to a game. Even if it is on TV, I feel obliged to go. It's an affliction."

Robertson was born in Petworth, West Sussex, dangerously close to Brighton, but his loyalties were assured when his father took him to see Pompey when he was about 12, and that was it.

"It was the side of the Fifties that was in decline from the glory days, but it still boasted legends such as Jimmy Dickinson, Jackie Henderson, and Peter Harris. My first two games were against Tottenham and Blackpool.

"I had never seen anything like it. It just hooked me and it has held me ever since. Redknapp has done brilliantly. I can't believe that success has come so quickly and that the team has knitted together so well. It's extraordinary. He was obviously wasted upstairs as director of football, it just didn't suit him.

"Take his signing of Todorov. Toddy took a few months to settle and it was a while before the crowd liked him, especially as he came in for Peter Crouch after he was sold to Aston Villa. He's not rumbustuous and we liked that at Fratton Park.

"There's a certain embattled spirit about the place, which used to draw everyone together. It was forged on grounds like Halifax and Port Vale, really unglamorous places where you would meet and see the same people every other week.

"I am slightly embarrassed that I am so obsessed with the club. No one quite understands it."

Robertson, who boasts he still has a fine sprout of hair, goes off on a little nostalgic reverie, listing his favourites – names that will mean nothing to anyone north of Petersfield: Ray Hiron, Colin Garwood, Kempy (David Kemp), Alan Biley and, "Oh, I nearly forgot, Ron Saunders."

He phoned me back: "I would have to put Peter Marinello (who signed for £150,000 in 1973) in the line up. I felt sorry for him having to put up with all the hype and being called the next George Best. He never made it and he was a terrible casualty. He was not a confident man and always looked hunched after a game, but he was a good lad."

Mick, who later ran the club phone hotline in those innocent pre-internet days, got to know many of the players of the Eighties well.

"I always had a beer with Paul Went after the game. He cost £150,000, which was a record, but he was injured almost immediately. I used to like Jeff Hemmerman and Archie Styles – I slept on his floor more than once.

"We had high hopes in the Eighties when John Deacon bought the place and promised so much, thinking he could buy success, but eventually it went wrong."

Indeed it did. Remember the Nineties?

ANORAK'S CORNER

September 7
Gillingham 1 Portsmouth 3
Scorers: Merson (29), Burchill (46), O'Neil (79)
Crowd: 8,797
Team: Hislop, Crowe (Harper), Taylor, De Zeeuw, Primus, Festa, Quashie, Hughes, Merson, Todorov, Burchill (O'Neil).
Substitutes: Kawaguchi, Vincent, Cooper.

Merson oversaw the third away win of the season with a definitive midfield performance, which saw him score one goal and create another for O'Neil. Gillingham's fight back was snuffed out by Burchill scoring on half time. Primus cleared off the line, Harper and O'Neil came on as subs, and it was the latter who scored the third, set up by Merson with 11 minutes left.

September 10
(Worthington Cup)
Portsmouth 2 Peterborough 0
Scorers: Quashie (26), Primus (76)
Team: Hislop, Crowe (Harper), Taylor, De Zeeuw, Primus, Festa, Quashie, Hughes (Pericard), Merson, Todorov, Burchill.
Substitutes: Kawaguchi, O'Neil, Robinson.

A muted performance by Pompey, a heroic struggle by the Third Division's bottom club. Merson created a goal in the 26th minute with a centre to Burchill, whose close-range shot rebounded on to the feet of Quashie and into goal. Defender Linvoy Primus scored from four yards in the 76th minute after a centre from Todorov.

September 14
PATIENCE OF A SAINT

I have a friend who supports St Mirren. His philosophy in football, though not in life, is to have few expectations. Assume your side will lose and you won't be disappointed when they do. If they win, savour the moment. That's how Portsmouth supporters have coped for years.

Now the expectations are unlimited. What can the average Pompey fan, weaned on failure out of disappointment, make of a team that is unbeaten and three points clear at the top of the First Division? In a report after last Saturday's game with Gillingham, I actually read these two adjectives describing the team's performance: attractive, effective. Attractive? Effective? Portsmouth?

When Alan Green's noisily inconsequential commentary on the England friendly was broken into with the news that Gillingham had pulled one back and that the game was "wide open", I knew with the certainty of a man well on the way to a cure of St Mirren's Syndrome (SMS) that it wasn't "wide open" at all and that Pompey would stroll it.

And so it proved, with Mighty Merse laying on a pass for the young, brilliant Gary O'Neil to score; 3-1, including a goal from Mark Burchill, the Scottish striker who, if Berti Vogts selected him, would score bucketloads of goals and save him from the sack. Hard to imagine that this is the same young man that Harry Redknapp, the manager, thought was too expensive when Graham Rix bought him for £600,000 last season.

A cup run of some sort is always good for SMS sufferers. Last year (and the one before, come to that; and the one before that), Milan Mandaric, the Portsmouth owner, demanded victory in the Worthington Cup. Sadly, mighty Colchester were too good. Exit in first round.

On another occasion, so woeful was the team in a drubbing at the hands of Blackburn Rovers that Mandaric gave the fans their money back. A perfect example of SMS came in the 1960-61 season. Pompey were living down to expectations in the old Second Division, managed by that quixotic (let's be charitable) character Freddie Cox. They surprised everyone with a jolly little run in the first season of the League Cup.

Pompey beat Coventry City, Manchester City and Chelsea – the city slickers, the *Daily Express* said – whose glamorous stars included a young Terry Venables. But just in case the fans got too carried away, they surrendered to Rotherham United in the fifth round.

One of the stars of that cup run was Dick Beattie, the goalkeeper who played a series of blinders – not least because he blacked up his eyes with coal dust to keep out the glare from the floodlights. He obviously understood how to cope with SMS by providing occasional flashes amid the dross. But then, he used to play for St Mirren.

In fact, it was the quintessential season for SMS sufferers: Pompey were relegated and knocked out of the FA Cup by Peterborough United, newly elected to the League.

So this week's 2-0 win in the Worthington Cup was a big step forward in rehabilitation from the SMS. Especially as the victim was that nemesis of old: Peterborough.

Nonetheless, just in case there is a recurrence of the complaint, Redknapp has warned fans that the club is in for a "belting" any time now but not, they hope, from Millwall today. The clubs have had an abrasive relationship since the two sets of fans hurled clinker at each other in a fight in the deeper, darker corners of south London in 1912. Last season, apart from a post-match punch-up at the away game, it was all sweetness with both sides chanting for Steve Claridge. He remains an authentic Pompey hero despite his cruel sacking two seasons ago and despite his pre-season prediction in the local paper that the best odds on Portsmouth going up were a mere 20-1. Obviously an SMS sufferer.

'Arry's Bargain Basement: the manager's hope of signing Fabrizio Ravanelli from Derby County has been dashed by Mandaric. Apparently, Redknapp had wangled a deal whereby Pompey paid £10,000-a-week wages for the striker, who is on £40,000, and Derby paid the balance. In effect, he was getting a rival to pay the club £30,000 a week. Now that really would have been a deal.

ANORAK'S CORNER

September 14
Portsmouth 1 Millwall 0
Scorer: Todorov (50)
Crowd: 17,201
Team: Hislop, Harper, Taylor, De Zeeuw, Primus, Festa, Quashie, Robinson (Tiler), Merson, Todorov (O'Neil), Pericard (Burchill).
Substitutes: Kawaguchi, Cooper.

Portsmouth celebrated their best-ever start to a season with Todorov's 50th-minute goal. Millwall played better in the first half, Kinet's shot was tipped over by Hislop in the opening seconds and Steve Claridge, old Pompey faithful, now Millwall striker, also forced a good save. It was all over when Quashie's through-ball caught out the Millwall defence and Todorov raced clear to score. Harry Redknapp said: "Our players are not used to being top and I thought we were a bit tense."

September 19
Portsmouth 4 Wimbledon 1
Scorers: Pericard (3), Todorov (31), og (38), Taylor (72)
Crowd: 18,837
Team: Hislop, Harper, Taylor, De Zeeuw, Primus, Festa, Quashie (O'Neil), Robinson, Merson, Todorov (Burchill), Pericard.

Substitutes: Kawaguchi, Tiler, Vincent.

Pompey took the lead in the third minute when one of those now-familiar long passes from Merson found Pericard. Wimbledon looked dangerous and equalised seven minutes later when McAnuff centred and Shipperley headed in. Todorov headed Portsmouth in front and then Wimbledon's Williams scored a spectacular own goal in the 38th minute with a powerful backpass, which easily beat the goalkeeper. To add insult, he was later sent off, leaving Taylor to round things off in the 72nd minute.

September 21

GOOD TIMES ROLL

You know times are good when Carl Tiler, one of the most mocked players in recent Portsmouth history, gets a warm welcome on his appearance as substitute. Everyone's a star if you're winning.

The joy of victory is all the better when one of the victims is Wimbledon – walloped 4-1 with the bonus of an "Enckelman" as Kelvin Davis repeated the Aston Villa goalkeeper's nightmarish error of the previous night. There hasn't been such fun since New Year's Day 1986 at Plough Lane when Mick Channon, who had been looking pretty jaded, plucked two goals out of nowhere in a 3-1 romp. Still, one almost felt sorry for the Wimbledon fans this week. They were outnumbered by 2,345 to one. There's a kind of heroism in such futility.

Enough gloating. Here are some statistics for Pompey fans planning trips to Liverpool and Manchester next season: not one of the sides in the top three at this stage last season were promoted; over the past five seasons, of the 15 clubs in the top three after nine games, only six went up.

On the other hand, three of the teams top at this stage – Fulham, Charlton and Sunderland – stayed there. And only

Fulham had acquired more points (nine wins out of nine) than Portsmouth (25 out of a possible 27).

Where that leaves us I'm not sure, but the chief football writer on the local paper, *The News*, has no doubt. Without a trace of bias, he describes these as "magical times".

There is a sense of pinch-me-it-can't-be-happening, magnified by this being a brand new team magicked up by manager Harry Redknapp during the summer when no one was looking. It's like turning up to an old mate's party in scruffy jeans, clutching a bottle of cider, only to find he's won the pools and all the guests are in black tie, drinking Bollinger.

There is still a sense of surprise, almost awe, that Paul Merson is actually a Portsmouth player. He's like some great Renaissance mercenary prince – a latter-day Francesco di Sforza doing battle for the Duke of Milan – sweeping all before him with a rapier thrust here, a cavalry charge there.

Yet it was Matthew Taylor, the attacking wing back, who walked away with the supporters' club's man-of-the-month award. Mighty Merse came third to Hayden Foxe, the uncompromising centre back who has been injured for four games.

Which brings us to Linvoy Primus. Everyone likes Linvoy because he has survived four managers in three years, gives 100 per cent, and, above all, because he is a familiar face. He clearly was not in Redknapp's plans but he is in the side because of injuries, first to Eddie Howe and now to Foxe. The defence of Primus, Gianluca Festa, who looks like an extra from *Reservoir Dogs* but more menacing, and Arjan De Zeeuw is impervious to most attacks thrown at them.

Primus said: "It was hard during the summer with all the new players coming in and realising that you probably weren't part of the first-team plans. Usually new managers bring in one or two players, not an influx like this."

Primus, 29, married with three children, aged from three weeks to eight years, has acquired the calm to cope because of a new-found belief in Christianity. "When things are wrong in my head, I read the Bible and fix myself on that," he said. "I have learnt that there is more to life than football. Now I go to Bible classes and I have learnt a lot about myself, and my life isn't going wrong any more".

More from 'Arry's Bargain Basement. He might have found a way round the transfer ban to bring in Tim Sherwood – he's had him in his sights so long the lad must think he's got a stalker – and Les Ferdinand, both from Spurs. But what Redknapp, banned for speeding this week, really needs is a chauffeur. How's a mover like 'Arry expected to do his deals without wheels?

ANORAK'S CORNER

September 21
Norwich 1 Portsmouth 0
Crowd: 21,335
Team: Hislop, Harper, Taylor, De Zeeuw, Primus, Festa, Quashie, Robinson (Ritchie), Merson, Todorov (Pericard), O'Neil (Burchill). Substitutes: Kawaguchi, Cooper.

Portsmouth's unbeaten league record came to an end in a fiercely contested match. In the first half, Hislop was kept the busier of the goalkeepers, bravely denying Mulryne a chance in the 30th. Merson and Taylor came close in the second half but Hislop was beaten by Iwan Roberts' header. Harry Redknapp, ever the philosopher, remarked: "You can't go on winning matches like we have; you'd end up with 125 points."

September 28
NEWS FROM THE HOME FRONT

I am indebted to The Blue Bazookas, a brass and blast ensemble from Portsmouth, who sent me their version of the *Pompey Chimes*. Very evocative. Very noisy. Let's hope the day jobs are just as invigorating. I'm afraid what really struck me was the commentary extract in very clipped pre-Wolstenholme tones on a 1950 game, which refers to the 'crowd of 50,000 certainly get their money's worth in this clash with Newport.'

50,000! The capacity at Fratton Park 52 years later is 19,179 giving it the sixth smallest capacity in the First Division (and that includes Brighton with their toy-town stadium of 6,960). When you think that Portsmouth were the first side to stage a floodlit game (in 1956 against Newcastle) and have a crowd record of 51,385, you wonder what's been happening for 32 years.

The truth is, there have been very few times in those long years when when the possibility of filling the ground week in week out was an issue. You could turn up a few minutes before kick off and get a good position in the North Stand, just behind the Mike Trebilcock fan club, without thinking of booking ahead.

Now, with promotion in the air, it's almost impossible to get into the place. Season tickets are at record sales, and if it goes on like this, the average gates will be about 5,000 more than last year.

Like so many old grounds, it's run down and rickety with stanchions that blot out great swathes of the pitch. But it's home. Amazingly, the South Stand was built in 1925 and there is still in existence one of the original turnstiles from the year of the club's formation in 1898. There have been attempts to move to a new stadium. The most recent, in 1992, was turned down because of the effect it would have on the wild geese on their migratory flight. Ironically, the geese no longer settle there. They have moved on, the club hasn't.

When Milan Mandaric bought the club in 1999, his promise that there would be a new 35,000-seater stadium was greeted with enthusiasm.

It is hard to work out what's been going on since. The council, more helpful than they have been in the past, have kept open an option on a chunk of the old rail goods yard that is being developed, but that option expires next month. There is talk of rebuilding the ground itself, but imagine the club in the Premiership with one side of the ground closed for redevelopment.

I had a quick click through the Pompey website to see where we were.

The issue has been the subject of a some testy exchanges between fans, the local paper and the various chief executives (six in all) who have worked with Mandaric.

On May 19 this year, the latest, Peter Storrie, said: "We have a number of sites under scrutiny and a fallback plan for the development of Fratton Park". He was "confident of a concrete statement in June."

On May 27, Mandaric said: "We are on track aggressively looking at all possibilities."

June 10, Peter Storrie is "confident of making a statement on June 30."

July 1, Peter Storrie: "Not far away from announcing plans."

July 22: "The announcement will be made before August 12."

July 23: "The announcment will be made between mid- and late-August."

You get the drift. Mention the word stadium to a Portsmouth fan and he wouldn't know whether to laugh or cry.

But whatever the politics and real-estate rows behind the scenes, it's an impossible decision to get right, even if there's enough cash in hand. When do you build the new stadium? Is there a right time?

Richard Whitehead, the man who knows more about football than you want to hear, said: "I hate to say this to Portsmouth supporters, but you need to look at the example of Southampton. For years they scraped by on a capacity crowd of 15,000. They build a new stadium (capacity 32,551) and suddenly find they have 10,000 extra fans. A bigger stadium is essential for long-term growth."

But look at Leicester. Expensive players, huge wage bill, a new stadium and relegation. So if Portsmouth get promoted this season, they won't have the crowds to support a team, and if they do build a stadium, will they be around long enough to cash in? Leicester, by the way, are averaging crowds of 27,953 this season to Portsmouth's 18,376.

Reading built a shiny new stadium in 1998 and were promptly relegated and played their first game in the Second Division.

As Richard Whitehead put it: "The only good time for Pompey to build a new ground would be in the next fortnight."

More from 'Arry's Bargain Basement. He's tracking Manchester City defender Paul Ritchie, still after Ravanelli and Tim Sherwood, and has been linked with Ashley Ward of Barnsley, but he did shift a Frenchman called Ulliano Courville who arrived a year ago and never even started one game.

ANORAK'S CORNER

September 28
Portsmouth 3 Bradford 0
Scorers: Quashie (17, 58), Pericard (21)
Crowd: 18,459
Team: Hislop, Harper, Taylor, De Zeeuw, Primus, Festa (Ritchie), Quashie, Robinson (O'Neil), Merson, Todorov (Burchill), Pericard. Substitutes: Kawaguchi, Cooper.

Kevin Harper and Svetoslav Todorov combined for Quashie to score with a fierce left-foot shot from 30 yards in the 17th minute, which went in off a post. Four minutes later, a Paul Merson special gave Pericard the chance to score. Another Merson pass split the defence in the 58th minute for Quashie to race on and hit his second.

October 1
Worthington Cup
Portsmouth 1 Wimbledon 3
Scorer: Pericard (6)
Crowd: 11,754
Team: Hislop, Harper, Taylor, Ritchie, Primus, Festa, O'Neil, Robinson, Merson, Todorov (Burchill), Pericard. Substitutes: Kawaguchi, Buxton, Tiler, Cooper.

Pericard put Pompey ahead but Wimbledon winger McAnuff equalised less than 60 seconds later. Leigertwood made it 2-1 after 15 minutes with a header, and Shipperley finished things off in the 58th.

CHAPTER 3
OCTOBER

October 5

THE ZOO BOY

The Pompey floor show is going nicely. First on, in a fetching grey tracksuit top and shorts, is Jim Smith (aka Eagle. As in Bald). Within 10 minutes he has gone red with the exertion of pumping up the players. He's the short, fat, hairy one. Come half time and enter the tall, sophisticated one, all suit and tie. That's Harry Redknapp, who comes down to the bench and stands, hand on chin, occasionally venturing to the touchline to remonstrate with his Blue Army. There's almost as much action as on the pitch. Quite a contrast to last season, when poor Graham Rix just stood there miserably chewing his nails.

As in all good music halls, the crowd have a song for them; Harry 'n' Jim, Harry 'n' Jim – as in the ditty that accompanies Rosie and Jim, the children's TV puppet characters.

Now they've coined a second verse. It goes: Oooh.

Even the drummer manages to come in with a beat, so the complete musical movement goes:

Harry 'n' Jim. Oooh, boom.

It's like the Last Night at The Proms.

It was more like Gotterdammerung on Tuesday, when Wimbledon and their 60 fans knocked Portsmouth out of the Worthington Cup after a display as drab and dreary as any last season. Paul Merson looked so bored that, after the game, at least two members of the supporters' club changed their votes for player of the month. How quickly oohs are replaced by boos. Now one of the favourites for the title is Arjan De Zeeuw, who is followed around by a strange booing sound. But it's not. It's an admiring "zoooooooo".

The Dutchman was a hero with Wigan Athletic, tasted Premiership life with Barnsley, and is now part of a sound defence with Gianluca Festa and Linvoy Primus. He was a classic Redknapp signing: he heard that the player was unhappy at Wigan and was on the phone with the speed of a heat-seeking missile.

De Zeeuw said: "I had refused to sign a new contract because I didn't think it was good enough. While I was holding out for something better, Harry phoned me. I asked him to wait while I was on holiday and he phoned the day I got back. I liked that. Harry's easy to talk to and makes you feel wanted. He leaves most of the day-to-day training to Jim Smith and Kevin Bond, but when he does suggest something, he is very adamant."

De Zeeuw, 32, was the fourth signing that Redknapp made one busy June week and he is surprised at how quickly the new team settled. "Sometimes it's harder when you are just the one person joining an established team, but this time we outnumbered the existing players," he said.

"Harry had told me he was going to make his own team, and, at the beginning in the pre-season friendlies, I wasn't sure how things were going to work out, especially losing to Chelsea and Celtic. We were a completely new defence, but there is a lot of experience, and, as soon as the season started, everything clicked.

"Now the players are happy, the fans are happy, and I think it does a lot for the community. People are always friendly when they see you in the street.

"We thought we might have a chance for the play-offs, but now I think automatic promotion is possible.

"But the Premiership is so different from the First Division. You can't make mistakes, it's so fast. The way Arsenal are playing is frightening. I like the example of Charlton, who are very organised, don't sign big names and stay within a sound system."

More from 'Arry's Bargain Basement. Pundits who talk about the crisis facing football should take a closer look at the Redknapp revolution. Everyone jokes about his wheeler-dealing but it is cleverer than that. He is playing a post-Digital game and winning by getting stars on a shoe string. So it looks as if he is going to get Fabrizio Ravanelli from Derby County, with them paying most of his wages, and he is talking to Ashley Ward of Bradford City. He fancies Jobi McAnuff and Damien Francis of Wimbledon. But they will cost money and as Redknapp said: "We won't be paying fees." To prove it, he has hired 28-year-old midfield player Lassina Diabate, who was born in the Ivory Coast and had been playing for Auxerre. On a Bosman, of course.

ANORAK'S CORNER

October 5
Rotherham 2 Portsmouth 3
Scorers: Pericard (15), Todorov (23), Merson (45)
Crowd: 8,604
Team: Hislop, Ritchie, Taylor, De Zeeuw, Primus, Festa, Quashie, Diabate, Merson, Todorov (Harper), Pericard.
Substitutes: Kawaguchi, O'Neil, Robinson, Burchill.

Pericard put Pompey ahead, then Todorov scored from a Taylor centre. *Rotherham pulled one back after 33 minutes when Byfield scored with a header. The first half ended in controversy when referee Graham Laws awarded Portsmouth a dubious penalty after Todorov went down in the area. Merson scored. Swailes of Rotherham was sent off for dissent. Rotherham scored again after 72 minutes when Alan Lee was tripped in the area by Festa and took the penalty himself. What really stole the show was Hislop being ordered to remove his lucky white cycle shorts, which he was wearing under his team shorts, because of a colour clash.*

October 12

FANS ACROSS THE SEA

Las Vegas. Why would you go to this gaudy, bawdy, sinful city? To see Olivia Newton-John at the Paris or Art Garfunkel at the Orleans? A little nostalgia with Neil Sedaka or Frank Sinatra Jr pretending to be his dad?

Be honest, it would be hard to resist the temptations of Cheetah's Topless Lounge or the showgirls at the Déjà Vu. It was the latter that proved too seductive for John Entwistle, guitarist for The Who, and he died in the arms of an exotic dancer (as they say in their trade) from that emporium.

For a small group of out-of-towners last weekend, none of these delights was enough to deflect them from their single-minded purpose. Not all the gambling tables on The Strip, not even the provocative charms of the Dreamgirls in the Olympic Gardens, could stop them fulfilling their dream – settling down in a hotel room and listening to a football match. Listening! Not even watching.

Clad in a shiny blue uniform with numbers on the back, they came from San Diego, from Florida, from Massachusetts and from New Jersey. Not for them Hunter S. Thompson-esque moments of fear and loathing. This was more beer and love-in.

They had come to listen to Rotherham United v Portsmouth for the first annual gathering of the US branch of the Portsmouth Supporters' Club.

Three days later and Steve Carthew-Burtcher ("don't ask me to explain the hyphen"), the founder, was still exhausted but happy. "What a weekend," he said. "We had a few shants (a south-coast word for pints), I can tell you. Absolutely hammered all the time."

It was by any standards surreal – almost as surreal as Paul Gascoigne being considered as manager of Exeter City, or Portsmouth being four points clear at the top of the First Division.

Steve quit his job as a plumber in Cosham, Portsmouth, and emigrated six years ago to San Diego, where he works on yacht maintenance. He found he was homesick for the club, for the camaraderie of away games and the nights in the pub afterwards.

He has recruited 70 members, including Norman Piper, a Pompey stalwart from the Seventies who coaches a San Diego side called the Delmar Sharks, and felt that a get-together was what they needed.

What the barmen in the MGM Grand Hotel Show Bar made of a 40-year-old man in Pompey colours bagging poolside seats by planting Pompey towels on them is unclear, but the Elvis impersonator in the bar loved every puzzled minute of it. Why else was he photographed draped in a six-foot square Pompey flag? So Elvis is a Pompey fan. Singing *A Mess of Blues*, presumably.

Steve, who has the shaven head and tattoos of a true Fratton Ender, said: "We turned the place into an English bar and made Elvis laugh. It was a bloody great hotel, about half the size of Portsmouth; they had a massive hockey game on in its arena, and lions in an enclosure behind a glass cage in the bar.

"What a weekend."

Not a lot like Fratton Park then, the place that has been the centre of his dreams since his first game, a 1976 cup match against Charlton Athletic. One-one draw with a goal by Piper. They lost the replay, of course.

"I set up the club so we could meet and talk about Pompey," Steve added. "This is just the first meeting of many. We plan to hold others in Florida and Graceland, New Orleans and I think there are four towns called Portsmouth in the States.

"But this was great. We took a load of beer to my room and listened to the Portsmouth radio station, Quay, via the computer. We also joined a chat room, so there were instant messages flying around from Dubai and Australia. The game was superb (a 3-2 win) but we had so much to drink, half of us were unconscious and missed the game, and one lad pulled a girl who looked like Mickey Quinn and was never seen again."

More from 'Arry's Bargain Basement. For the first time this season, not one rumour has leaked out about an impending Redknapp coup. So watch the papers for any player coming to the end of his contract, being dropped from the first team, or having a row with the boss. He could be in the side for next week's game with Coventry City.

October 19

EAST GOES WEST

Every club has that moment of self-deluded madness when it tries to cheer up the fans by chucking lots of money at some never-will-be-any-good player. It's usually some flash forward. Few Pompey fans will forget Mike Trebilcock, who scored two fabulous goals in the 1966 Cup Final for Everton against Sheffield Wednesday then disappeared into their reserves, only to be resurrected by Portsmouth.

He scored on his debut against Derby County with a speculative shot, which, amazingly, went in. It was downhill all the way after that. What a tarradiddle was made of Peter Marinello, the poor man's George Best. Apart from the hair, he was very poor. I was reminded this week of Ian Baird in the Eighties. Aaaarrrgghh.

Goalkeepers don't usually attract quite that flash and cash. Portsmouth have had some sterling custodians: Norman Uprichard in the Fifties, John Milkins in the Sixties and Alan Knight for ever. And now there is Yoshi Kawaguchi. It's hard to see him as anything other than a victim of the cruel commercial world of modern football. There he was happily plying his trade for Yokohama F-Marinos in Japan, he had been in goal at the World Cup in 1998 and he was one of the country's biggest pin-ups. Girls swooned, so did boys.

Websites were set up not only in Japan but also Thailand and Malaysia to talk about his cute smile and his boyish good looks. Then Harry Redknapp, in his days as director of football, came visiting. The reasoning was simple: buy the most popular player in Japan and all the fans in the Far East will be wearing Pompey gear. At £39.99 a shirt, that could be quite a nice earner. Well, it was more complicated than that, but you get the drift.

It made the £1.8 million investment and the contract for

£340,000 over three years seem worthwhile even if it did make the 26-year-old easily the most expensive player signed by Portsmouth.

Kawaguchi arrived a year ago this weekend to a tumultuous welcome from Japanese fans and press. Fratton Park was like a giant sushi bar. At the Millwall game last season, the Japanese press corps almost outnumbered locals. They were a little muted after Yoshi, with what had become his trademark flap at high centres, presented the ball to Richard Sadlier, the Millwall striker, for an easy goal.

There were a few cynics. The correspondent for the *Mainichi Daily News* in Japan wrote: "I hope this move comes off because that will bring money to Yokohama and Portsmouth – even if he has to warm the bench all season."

Graham Rix, then the Portsmouth manager, displayed his usual lack of enthusiasm at anything that appeared to emanate from Milan Mandaric, the chairman, and insisted that everyone had to justify their place in the team.

The problem was that Yoshi never played well enough. In 13 games, he let in 25 goals and hasn't made a start since March when Leyton Orient knocked Pompey out of the Cup 4-1. He was replaced by the ancient Dave Beasant. Shirt sales have not rocketed.

When he arrived, Mandaric said: "Bringing Yoshi to the club means we are moving forward on the field and bringing an international dimension to this beautiful city." In January, he said it was in Yoshi's interests "to go back to Japan". The fans sense he hasn't had much of a deal.

It's difficult interviewing him because his English isn't good. (There was a splendid moment last season when he and the Italian, Alessandro Zamperini, stood in the goalmouth trying to discuss tactics – each in their own language.) His agent told me that "no", he isn't at all disappointed not playing first-team football, and "no", he is not dwelling on the past, just trying to regain his place.

He did feel, perhaps, that he hadn't been given enough of a chance to take stock of the game and the culture at a time when the team was shipping goals. He is, his agent said, a realist biding his time. It may be a long wait with Shaka Hislop looking so comfortable. So the man who was greeted with a cheery cry of "banzai" every time he took a goal kick now sits on the bench under the heading: Subs not used.

More from 'Arry's Bargain Basement. Well less, actually. For the second consecutive week, not one player has been linked to the club, which is a world record.

ANORAK'S CORNER

October 19
Portsmouth 1 Coventry 1
Scorer: Pericard (50)
Crowd: 18,837
Team: Hislop, O'Neil (Ritchie), Taylor, De Zeeuw, Primus, Festa, Quashie, Diabate, Merson, Todorov (Burchill), Pericard.
Substitutes: Kawaguchi, Harper, Robinson.

Pericard scored his fourth in four games, chipping past the Coventry keeper after collecting a fine pass from (who else?) Paul Merson. Davenport scored 16 minutes into the second half after a mis-tackle by Primus. Hislop kept the unbeaten home record intact in the 80th minute with a brilliant save.

October 26

A SENSE OF HISTORY

One of the clever things Milan Mandaric did when he bought Portsmouth three years ago was recognise the power of the fans. Maybe it's been the cleverest thing he has done. He realised, like many others who have visited Fratton Park, as opposition players or fans, that the passion of the support is in direct disproportion to the degree of success.

Of course, all clubs think they have the monopoly on fan power, but it was striking how mute the Crystal Palace home fans were earlier this season, even when they were 2-0 up at half time. Last season at Watford, when the home team was winning 3-0, the Pompey end, rightly disdainful of the Hornets fans' inability to raise even a buzz of approval, adapted *Pompey Chimes* for a few rousing choruses of *Play Up Watford*. The fans helped end years of bad stewardship by rallying for the appointment of Terry Venables, and then helped bring him low when they realised he was not quite the ticket. I said they were enthusiastic, not prescient.

Mandaric has played on the fans' loyalty with great success. He buys the regulars pints in the Newcome Arms and decreed that the No. 12 shirt should be dedicated to the Pompey Fan. Some of the fans pay him uncritical tribute for buying the club out of administration. Others, more sceptically – given his volatile record of hiring and firing managers and directors – reckon that one chorus of "There's only one Milan" (to the tune of *Blue Moon*) per match is quite enough adulation, thank you.

Whatever goes on in the boardroom or on the pitch, the fans go on forever. Take Richard Owen. He is the club's historian, but he is more than that. He supports the club with unswerving commitment.

His grandfather went to his first Portsmouth game in 1912

and took his son to watch the great side of the Forties and early Fifties. Owen, in turn, was taken to see his first game on December 28, 1965, but he was only six at the time and too young to be hooked. He did not return to Fratton Park until 1972, and his interest really began with the formation of the SOS campaign in 1977 to help to raise funds for the club as it started its inexorable plunge to the Fourth Division.

Ian St John was manager, then Jimmy Dickinson, the most capped player in Pompey history, took over, only to die six months later. Richard said: "Jimmy was too nice. Did you know he was never booked? We raised cash with street appeals and by selling old newspapers at £1 a ton."

Then, considering that the programme was poor, he wrote to the club to say he could do better. He became assistant editor and, by the time of Alan Ball's first reign in the 1980s, became the club's official historian. This is serious stuff. Owen has between 5,000 and 6,000 programmes neatly lined up in his detached house in a Havant cul-de-sac. He has the 1939 Cup Final programme for what was a memorable and unexpected 4-1 win over Wolverhampton Wanderers. He even has a rosette and a match ticket. He has watched Portsmouth play on 105 league grounds and missed only five games since 1984.

What he wants above all is to create a museum of Portsmouth memorabilia and he is working on a volume of Pompey's 100 best players. His all-time best three: Jack Froggatt, a wing half from the Forties and Fifties; Ron Saunders, the granite-faced centre forward who scored even in bad times and went on to be an uncompromising manager; and Guy Whittingham, who scored 47 goals in the 1992-93 season.

Owen said: "I was always an admirer of Mick Tait, who played in ten different shirts and gave 1,000 per cent during his time in the Eighties."

I tried him on three questions from my small collection of

Pompey programmes.

Who played inside left for Spurs in the 1967 Cup tie?

Who scored on his debut against Derby County in 1967?

Which Portsmouth player had a second spell for the club in 1981?

Richard got them all. (Answers below.)

More from 'Arry's bargain basement. This one might have passed manager Redknapp by. Peter Harris, one of the great post-war players in the country and not just for Portsmouth, is about to auction his memorabilia. The club should buy it. And put it in Owen's museum.

Quiz answers: Terry Venables; Mike Trebilcock; Chris Kamara.

ANORAK'S CORNER

October 26

Burnley 0 Portsmouth 3

Scorers: Quashie (21), Todorov (58), Harper (86)

Crowd: 15,788

Team: Hislop, Stone, Taylor, De Zeeuw, Primus, Ritchie, Quashie, Diabate (Robinson), Merson, Todorov (Harper), Pericard.

Substitutes: Kawaguchi, O'Neil, Burchill.

Burnley had not lost since August yet were routed by a Portsmouth inspired by Steve Stone, making his loan debut from Aston Villa, who gave them the penetration they have lacked on the right and the perfect balance to Taylor on the left. Merson tucked in behind Pericard and Todorov, and between them – and with a lot of help from an in-form Quashie – they dominated Burnley. At one point, Pompey put together 21 passes. In the last ten minutes, Pericard had a header saved, Ritchie hit the post and Robinson had a shot cleared off the line. Redknapp was so thrilled at the end of the game, he left the dugout to salute his happy fans.

October 29
Portsmouth 3 Preston 2
Crowd: 18,585
Scorers: Stone (23), Merson (26 pen), Taylor (34)
Team: Hislop, Stone, Taylor, De Zeeuw, Ritchie, Festa, Quashie, Diabate, Merson, Todorov (O'Neil), Pericard (Harper).
Substitutes: Kawaguchi, Primus, Burchill.

Preston went ahead in the 12th minute with a Cresswell goal but Stone, on a month's loan from Aston Villa, levelled in the 23rd. Merson scored from the penalty spot after a foul on Pericard. Taylor scored the third goal just before half time. Forty seconds after the re-start, Preston's Alexander scored a penalty after Ritchie fouled Rankine.

CHAPTER 4

NOVEMBER

November 2
SELLING TO SURVIVE

It's not looking good. The club shop has run out of Pompey Beanie Babies. The demand for the cuddly little chaps – made by Ty, the toy firm that is the club's sponsor – has been so intense that the initial order of 7,000 has been snapped up and they just can't make them fast enough to meet demand. Just think of all those weeping children this Christmas.

Still, there are compensations. It looks like Portsmouth won't be relegated this season; only 12 more points to reach the 'safe' total of 50. Or, to put it another way, at this stage of the season in the past five years no team has scored as many goals, notched up as many points or been so far ahead in the Nationwide League First Division. Phew.

The true Pompey fan, a pessimist to the core, will still be worrying about relegation – from the Premiership. Even the most cautious reckons the club will be promoted but remembers 1987, when Portsmouth went up to the old First Division only to go straight down again.

LOAN STAR: Classy, clever, deceptive. Vincent Pericard, on loan from Juventus, scored on his debut and wrecked Reading in April.

HAPPY RETURN: Deon Burton (above) scored on his return to Fratton Park after a six-year absence but faded as the season progressed.

PLAYMAKER: Paul Merson (left) could see the gaps in defences and exploit them in a way not seen by Pompey fans for years.

ZOO BOY: *Arjan de Zeeuw became a firm favourite, his every move greeted with an affectionate 'zoooo'.*

GOOD LUCA: Controlled, unruffled, Gianluca Festa did not put a foot wrong all season (apart from that pass in the Sheffield Wednesday game).

SHARPER:. Kevin Harper was the target of boos earlier this season but his foraging runs won the fans over.

MASTERMINDS

Clockwise from the top left: Manager Harry Redknapp, coach Kevin Bond, chairman Milan Mandaric and assistant manager Jim Smith.

ON HIS TODDY: *After a lacklustre start last season, Svetoslav Todorov proved himself an instinctive goalscorer.*

Will they survive the Premiership? Of course they will, with Harry Redknapp picking up brilliant waifs and strays such as Paul Merson for next to nothing, and the likes of Steve Stone on loan. The arrival of second-placed Leicester City today is a stark reminder that sound finances are as important as sound players.

Portsmouth do not like Leicester. David Follows, of Wilmslow, Cheshire, who reproved me for saying Jack Froggatt was a wing half when he was, in fact, in the centre, pointed out that if Leicester, then bottom of the old Second Division, had not beaten mighty Pompey in the 1949 FA Cup semi-final, the club might have won the Double.

No one can forget the pain inflicted by Leicester in the play-offs in 1993, when a "definite" offside goal by Ian Ormondroyd robbed the club of a stab at promotion. Now, newly relegated, they are in deep financial trouble, with debts of up to £50 million. Portsmouth are the division's fourth-most frugal club with a balance of £900,000 – thanks, in part, to the sale of Peter Crouch to Aston Villa for £5.5 million last season.

But... the wage bill is up 26 per cent and now stands at more than £7 million a year. Crucially, gates are at the highest level since 1968-69, when they averaged 16,500. Last season it was 14,700, now it's a fortnightly sell-out of 18,000 plus, which works out at about £1.10 million more a season in the kitty. If the club had its share of the ITV Digital cash, it would be within £500,000 or so of breaking even.

The Digital fiasco could be a blessing – however heavily disguised. Paul Rawnsley, sports business consultant of Deloitte & Touche, which produces an annual audit on the state of football, sees a window of opportunity for clubs to get their finances in order.

"There is now a mood of greater realism," Rawnsley said. "The transfer market is slowing down. Clubs and organisations such as the PFA are looking at performance-related pay, offering a smaller basic wage with bonuses linked to how club or player performs. Some are considering contracts which allow wage cuts when the club gets relegated."

These are remote issues when your team is flying. Success breeds excess. An astonishing 21,000 Pompey kits have been sold – the cheapest sell at £35 – and more local businesses are advertising their wares on hoardings around the ground than ever. Take Capileo, a tattooist and body-piercing firm, which advertises its distinctive products. Its owners have noted an upswing in business and Mark Libby (16 or 17 pierced bits), the co-owner, reckons it has been a good investment.

He said: "We get a lot of requests for a 'Made in Pompey' tattoo around the belly button, but we won't do names or logos. Too many people want them changed back and it's too painful and too diffficult."

I can understand him being impatient at men who want to replace "I love Ethel" with "Kiss me Kylie" but he is overlooking one essential fact: men are far more faithful to their club than their women.

More from 'Arry's Bargain Basement. Nicking Stone from Graham Taylor at Aston Villa was a coup. So was selling Crouch to him – despite the anguish it caused fans at the time. If you stuck the £3.5 million profit from the striker's sale in a savings account at 4.4 per cent, it would bring in more than £2,500 a week. That would just about pay the petrol bill for Merson's daily commute from St Albans.

ANORAK'S CORNER

November 2
Portsmouth 0 Leicester 2
Crowd: 19,107
Team: Hislop, Stone, Taylor, De Zeeuw, Primus, Festa (Ritchie),

Quashie, Diabate (O'Neil), Merson, Todorov (Burchill), Pericard.
Substitutes: Kawaguchi, Harper.

The ground was utterly waterlogged, but despite the pools of water that were to make play impossible, the referee ruled the game could go ahead. A muscular Leicester adapted better to the conditions and scored twice in the first half to narrow the gap between the two top teams to three points. Harry Redknapp said: "The match should never have been allowed to go ahead. It was nonsense, crazy. I told my players at half time just to kick the ball forward, so what type of football is that?"

November 6
Wolves 1 Portsmouth 1
Scorer: Merson (56)
Crowd: 27,022
Team: Hislop, Stone, Taylor, Ritchie, Primus, Robinson (Harper), Quashie, Diabate (O'Neil), Merson, Todorov (Burchill), Pericard.
Substitutes: Kawaguchi, Cooper.

A marvellous goal from Merson, lifting his free kick over the wall gave Portsmouth the lead in the 56th minute. Six minutes later, Dean Sturridge for Wolves saw off three Portsmouth defenders before sliding the ball past Hislop.

November 9
A WORD FROM THE FANS

It's obvious, I suppose, but when the team are winning, the fans are wittier, nicer to old ladies and policemen, and more tuneful. The moment they lose, they revert to throwing beer cans at the police and insulting their dogs, like they did after the Leicester City defeat last week, and singing hate-songs about S**th*mpt*n.

I've always found the anti-S**nts chants rather depressing,

probably because they are more to do with what is happening on the pitch than any personal animus against Portsmouth's more successful rivals. The worse the performances, the louder the chants of "stand up if you hate the scum" and the more unrelenting the abuse showered on any one-time "scummer" playing for the opposition. Still, if you are losing 1-0 to Grimsby Town and relagation is beckoning, it does help to ease the pain and tension. Scum, for the PhDs in the Fratton End, comes from ancient Teutonic languages and is a brewing term: "a film formed upon stagnant, foul water", the Oxford English Dictionary says.

It turns up in Marlowe, Shakespeare and Shelley as the "lowest class of the population of a place or country". More pleasing, for those whose hatred of the said club runs deep, skummer (I know the spelling's not quite right) is "the dung of a dog or a fox".

Anyway, after last Saturday's game – I use the word loosely; Nelson could have launched his fleet on the drenched pitch – I found myself with a S**th*mpt*n fan. Seemed quite a decent cove. I hadn't realised that they also use scummer to insult Portsmouth. Most insulting, they just ignore them – for Southampton have been in football's top flight since 1978 and Portsmouth scarcely rate a thought.

Now that the fans have the confidence you would expect from a side five points clear at the top of the Nationwide League First Division, the anti-scum chants have been replaced by cheery little tributes to manager Harry Redknapp's revolution such as:

When we are promoted,
This is what we'll sing,
We are Portsmouth,
We are Portsmouth,
Harry is our king.

...proving the poet Byron spot on when he wrote "all convulsion ends in rhyme".

Success usually makes the management more mellow too, so I felt a twinge of sympathy for the D**ly T*l*gr*ph writer who has been banned by the club for, er, irony.

Clubs and journalists are always falling out. The club bans them for some misdemeanour – i.e., daring to be critical – and the paper ripostes by splashing the ban over its front page and staging elaborate pictures of its reporter in the crowd, clutching notebook. Portsmouth's evening paper, *The News*, was banned all this summer for its apparent hostility but the trickiest time came in the Venables era of the mid-Nineties when he boycotted the paper for exposing uncomfortable truths about his management team.

All it did was guarantee unfriendly coverage – particularly poignant since the paper had been the official sponsor – and the chief football writer had to smuggle himself into the ground. But revenge is sweet: El Tel staged a ceremony for the start of work on the new stand without inviting *The News*. As the formalities got underway, a cherry picker hove into view above the Fratton End – complete with photographer.

The D**ly T*l*gr*ph's sin was to joke that Harry Redknapp had avoided the sack by bouncing back from defeat at Norwich with the 3-0 win over Bradford. Milan Mandaric, the chairman, was not amused.

As anyone close to Portsmouth knows, Harry doesn't qualify for the Chairman's Traditional Vote of Confidence until he has completed the average tenure for a Pompey manager under Mr M, which is eight months. That's not until mid-December.

So forget irony, the only way is a straight insult. I called Mandaric a disaster for sacking Steve Claridge as player-manager, and was summoned for a chat. The great philanthropist was charm itself, with cups of coffee all round, and the offer of lunch in the boardroom. Still waiting for that, by the way, although a Pukka Pie and a pint of Tetley's in the supporters' club goes a long way to compensate.

More from 'Arry's Bargain Basement. Taribo West, the Nigerian formerly with Derby County, is in training. A born-again Christian, he was sacked from 1FC Kaiserslautern because he went AWOL on a preaching mission. Be ready for a chorus of "stand up if you love the Saints..."

ANORAK'S CORNER

November 9
Derby 1 Portsmouth 2
Scorers: Todorov (27), Burchill (51)
Crowd: 26,587
Team: Hislop, Stone, Taylor, De Zeeuw, Primus, Ritchie (Foxe), Quashie, Diabate, Merson, Todorov (Harper), Burchill (Pericard). Substitutes: Kawaguchi, Robinson.

Derby scored after 16 minutes when Diabate's challenge on Lee Morris resulted in a penalty. Merson and Quashie then took control of midfield but it was a Todorov exchange with Taylor that led to the Bulgarian scoring. Six minutes into the second half, fast passing between Stone, Quashie and Merson reached Taylor, whose cross found Burchill unmarked and ready with his head.

November 16
GONE TO THE CRICKET

For a boy who dreamt of stardom, it all started so well. Rory Allen signed for Tottenham Hotspur when he was 14 and became a professional when he was 17. After 33 games, he became the most expensive player in Portsmouth's history when

Alan Ball signed him in 1999 for about £1 million.

He looked the part, scoring two goals in five starts, and, as Ball recalls: "He was a young boy with lots of potential, a super lad who was good in training and wide-eyed about football."

And then, though no one could have realised it at the time, the dream was over. He broke his ankle, made a comeback three months later and broke the other ankle. His career with Portsmouth reads: ten games, three goals and eight operations on knee and ankles. He hasn't played in a competitive game since May 2000 – 920 days ago.

Last week, aged 25, he threw in the towel, chucked away £3,000 a week, left a resignation note for the chief executive and went off to watch the cricket in Australia. "He's barmy," *The Sun* headlined.

Exit, to cheap gibes, a young man who once seemed to have so much.

As Ball told me: "It was a sad day when I heard what he had done. He wanted to be a really good player. He had the look. When he was injured, it was a cruel blow but he was far too brave for his own good.

"It is hard enough staying 100 per cent fit as a professional footballer but just imagine how it was for him with horrific injuries like that. It is all too easy to forget how ordinary people feel when they injure themselves – it really brings you down.

"I saw him not long ago and he was hoping and praying that he could get better. He was still living the dream."

Even when Allen was the guest of the supporters' club in September, he was still clinging to the dream. He told the fans that his personal goals were to "get fit and play football and hopefully impress Mr Redknapp enough to earn another contract".

Paddy Thomas, chairman of the supporters' club, saw a man

who "had gone through footballer's hell. He was very down at the time. He came over as someone who had been very depressed and I thought he had begun to think he would never play again. It's a real shame. He did have a striker's ability but people had begun to look askance at him and wonder what was going on. The meeting seemed to cheer him up though, he thought he was going to be given a rough ride by the supporters but they were very sympathetic."

There was little sympathy when, two years ago, he was arrested for being drunk and disorderly, and was fined by the club. Instead of seeing a lad in torment, the fans saw a lout in trouble and they grew impatient. This season, manager Harry Redknapp, who had been publicly supportive, warned that there "could be real problems ahead for the lad if he doesn't get fit and get some matches under his belt".

One official at the club suggested to me that his injuries were "all in the mind".

Maybe they were, but as Keith Waldon, assistant manager to Ball at the time of the transfer and now vice-chairman of the Society of Sports Therapists, said: "People forget that psychological damage often accompanies physical injuries. The hurt can stay in the mind long after the actual injury has healed.

"When I heard that he had been done for drinking, my thought was that that was not the behaviour of the boy I remember. He's not a bad lad, in fact, he's very intelligent.

"I don't think he should give up just yet. He needs the right kind of handling. I would work on his confidence, set him little goals, and, when he achieved one, then try him with another and so on."

Here's what the local paper, *The News*, said about Allen in its coverage of a friendly game in July: "If anything, he looked sharper than at any point during his ten games in a Pompey shirt. Allen was hungry, his touch superb and his finishing exquisite." Or as Waldon recalls: "I thought we had a superstar on our hands."

More from 'Arry's Bargain Basement. Well, I suppose the £3,000 saved on Allen's wages could go towards prising Fabrizio Ravanelli from Derby but what the team really needs is another defender with Eddie Howe, Gianluca Festa and Paul Ritchie all injured.

ANORAK'S CORNER

November 16
Portsmouth 3 Stoke City 0
Scorers: Burchill (49), Pericard (87), Todorov (93)
Crowd: 18,701
Team: Hislop, Harper (Crowe), Taylor, De Zeeuw, Primus, Foxe, Quashie, Diabate, Merson, Todorov (O'Neil), Burchill (Pericard). Substitutes: Kawaguchi, Robinson.

Stoke had the better of an uninspiring first half, with goalkeeper Hislop twice denying City striker Tommy Mooney with fine saves. Pompey did not have to wait long for the opening goal, which came four minutes into the second half when Burchill fired home the opener from a Kevin Harper cross. Substitute striker Pericard scored with a header three minutes from time. Todorov hit number three in stoppage time.

November 23
GOLDEN EAGLE

Whatever happened to McFadden and Whitehead? The sound of the satin-clad, loon-panted duo played the fans out of Fratton Park last week after the undoing of Stoke with:

Ain't no stoppin' us now, we're on the move,

Ain't no stoppin' us now, we're in the groove.

Certainly felt like it. For long, achingly frustrating periods, Pompey were forced to pass the ball around in a dour attempt to unlock the 27-man Stoke defence. When they did, it was thanks to a fine run by Kevin Harper, who had been cruelly booed by the crowd at the start of the match, and a cross dazzlingly converted by Mark Burchill. Maybe manager Harry Redknapp, who thought the striker wasn't worth the £600,000 Graham Rix paid, is warming to him.

The two other goals were like little Klondike moments in an otherwise grey day. Paul Merson's delicate scissor-kick to the eager feet of Svetoslav Todorov was a joy. Seven points clear. As Andy, from the Pompey Anoraks, and I agreed on the train back to London: you had to pinch yourself to be sure it was really happening.

But Redknapp has found a dark lining to the silver clouds. He reckons he is two players short – he has been saying that all season, although this time he is right – and is desperate to strengthen his injury-ravaged squad. "We'll never get this chance again. If we don't make it this year, forget it," he said. But the fans are brimming with optimism, not least Mick Quinn, as portly now as he was when he scored 22 goals in 1987, a year Portsmouth were promoted to the old Division One.

"If you look at the squad and compare it player for player, pound for pound, with the other sides in the division, they are by far the best," he said. "You see quality everywhere: there's

Merson, who makes a 40-yard pass land on a sixpence, Nigel Quashie is better than he was last season and his shooting is far more accurate, and Steve Stone has given the balance to the midfield."

And there's Redknapp's oldest signing, the indefatigable Bald Eagle, Jim Smith. Now 62, he is back as assistant manager and brings all the fire he brought to Colchester United (promoted), Birmingham City (promoted), Oxford United (promoted twice), Queens Park Rangers (League Cup finalists), Newcastle United (play-offs) and Derby County (promoted) and in between, in the early 1990s, he got Pompey to the FA Cup semi-finals and to the play-offs. He also bought Quinn from Pompey when he was at Newcastle.

"Jim's a man's man," Quinn said. "If you get it wrong and annoy him, he will give you a good bollocking, but he will praise you when you deserve it. He will tell you to your face when you are dropped, you won't read about it first in the paper. He likes 100 per cent players and he is not interested in the ones who play brilliantly for an hour. Jim was going to bring me back to Pompey from Coventry. The deal was all wrapped up when he phoned me to say he had been sacked."

The difference between Smith and Redknapp is clear from their double act in the dugout. There's Smith, all baseball cap, rumpled grey shorts and anorak, cajoling, shouting, straining at the leash, while Redknapp, all suit and silk tie, is as cool as James Bond facing his first Martini of the day.

"When Harry persuaded Jim to come back to Portsmouth, it raised a few eyebrows," Quinn said. "Then it all made sense because they bounce off each other so well, with Harry's wheeler-dealing and Jim's motivational skills." Quinn, who now works on a local radio station and trains horses, has put his money on promotion, but how does today's team compare with his? "I would say this side has better ball skills, but we had the hard edge, with Billy Gilbert, Noel Blake and Mick Tait. We had raw aggression. But we'll have to see if they are promoted before we compare them."

What does he mean "if"?

More from 'Arry's Bargain Basement. So far he has played 22 players, compared with the 19 who saw Alan Ball's team up in 1987, but he is still on at chairman Milan Mandaric to add to the wage bill. His latest target? Could be Arsenal's Ray Parlour. As McFadden and Whitehead went on to advise: don't let nothing stand in your way ay ay.

ANORAK'S CORNER

November 23
Sheffield Wednesday 1 Portsmouth 3
Scorers: Todorov (2), O'Neil
Crowd: 16,602
Team: Hislop, Harper, Taylor, De Zeeuw, Primus (Crowe), Foxe, Robinson, Diabate, Merson (O'Neil), Todorov (Burchill), Pericard.
Substitutes: Kawaguchi, Pitt.

Leading scorer Todorov took his league tally to nine in the eleventh minute. Merson limped off after 25 minutes following two fierce tackles by Wednesday players. Wednesday levelled two minutes later. Substitute Gary O'Neil replaced Merson and played with great assurance, proving that the team could function without the great man. He nearly equalised after 31 minutes but goalkeeper Pressman saved brilliantly. It was Todorov who restored Portsmouth's lead in the 52nd minute after a slick move involving O'Neil and Pericard. Todorov's cross in the 63rd minute found Pericard, who squared the ball to O'Neil, who scored.

November 30

FANTASTIC MR FOXE

There's something about Australians that makes Portsmouth fans splutter into their Gales. That something is Terry Venables, who watched while the club drifted into penury. Tel was hailed as a saviour when he became a consultant in 1996, then chairman and ultimately owner, but things turned nasty when he became national coach of the Australia team.

He and his sidekick, Terry Fenwick, felt they had to journey frequently Down Under checking on players, and soon they started turning up in Pompey shirts. No less than seven, to be precise.

Only one of them, John Aloisi, appeared to have kicked a football before, scoring 12 goals in the 1996-97 season, but fans still thrill (with horror) to the memory of Robbie Enes and Craig Foster, not to mention the 'goalkeeper', Zeljko Kalac, and two strikers – Hamilton Thorp and Paul Harries. Harries was so hopeless that he wouldn't have been given a game in a Sunday league side on a wet Tuesday. When he came on as a substitute against Bournemouth, he was so bad that he, in turn, had to be substituted.

As the team hurtled to what seemed inevitable relegation, Venables hot-footed it back to the safety of the TV studio. Leeds United fans might take encouragement from that. But now there's Foxey. Here's an Aussie the fans do care a XXXX about. He was Harry Redknapp's first signing in the summer bargain hunt, and, unlike the Aussies who came before, he's good. In fact, Richard Owen, the club historian, puts Hayden Foxe above stalwarts such as Phil Gunter, Colin Blant, Paul Went and Darren Moore, a more recent favourite.

Last Saturday, after the 3-1 stroll against Sheffield Wednesday, when Redknapp did his traditional grumble about lack of resources, he groaned that he had only one central defender fit to play but remarked wryly that it didn't really matter because "Foxey can do it by himself". It probably seems perverse to say that a side that has scored 44 and conceded 18 has struggled in defence but Foxe, 25, has all the attributes that a promotion side needs: positional sense, sound tackling and cool.

His return to the side two weeks ago, after two months out with a torn hamstring, was greeted with a mighty cheer. He was also the easiest of Redknapp's signings to recognise when the team was first paraded in August – tall and red-headed, towering above his team-mates. So with four of the defence injured, who will be alongside him in defence today against wilting Walsall?

"I don't know, mate. I guess it'll be me, me and me. I can't guess what Harry has got up his sleeve, but he'll have something; he'll know what to do, mate," Foxe said.

"Harry doesn't bullshit; when he asked me to join, he said he wanted to have a right go this year and that he was going to bring in a lot of new faces. He brought in players that adapted to his system.

"He doesn't muck about you know, mate." Redknapp signed Foxe previously when he was at West Ham United and the player made the headlines more for his boozy escapades than his football – he was fined £12,000 for distinctly leery behaviour in a nightclub.

"Harry got me out of the poo, mate. This is a great chance for me. It has been great to get away from London and I learnt that sometimes you have to take a step back to move forward. I've changed my lifestyle. I'm Aussie, mate, I'll always like a drink, but now I know when it's the right time to have a beer."

Now, he's enjoying the quiet life on the south coast with Fabianne, his French wife. "It's so quiet, mate, it's green and sunny.

"We love it down here," he said. "This is the best time of my career – though, of course, when you're winning, everything feels good; it's a feeling which lasts all through the week. It's wonderful for the fans and for us, mate. Everyone is in a good mood."

You're right there, mate.

More from 'Arry's Bargain Basement. Taribo West, the eccentric born-again Christian and former AC Milan defender, has been signed on a free but Redknapp has dismissed reports about Steve Davis, the Burnley centre half, and Alexander Mostovoi, Celta Vigo's Russia midfield player. But, where there's smoke...

Ernandes da Silva, the 20-year-old son of Mirandinha, the Brazilian who dazzled at Newcastle United, is also on trial. Didn't Jim Smith have Dad in his side back in the 1980s?

The biggest boost to Redknapp's buying power has been the sale of 2,300 additional season tickets in two weeks. That's an injection of £300,000 or so – very handy for the January sales.

ANORAK'S CORNER

November 30
Portsmouth 3 Walsall 2
Scorers: Quashie (45), Todorov (58), Taylor (76)
Crowd: 17,701
Team: Hislop, Harper, Taylor, Crowe, Ritchie, Foxe, Quashie, Diabate, Merson (O'Neil), Todorov (Buxton), Pericard (Burchill). Substitutes: Kawaguchi, Pitt.

A doughty performance from Walsall, who took the lead with a penalty after 30 minutes. Quashie equalised right on half time and although Portsmouth took the lead with a Todorov goal, they failed to impress. Sonner was brought down in the penalty area and scored his second. Portsmouth went ahead in the 74th minute when

Todorov gave Taylor the chance to score from three yards. A fine stop from Hislop in the 87th minute saved the day – one characterised by disappointing play and the booking of six players.

CHAPTER 5

DECEMBER

December 7

HIRON FIRE

For once the crowd in the North Stand were ahead of the Fratton End with a quick chorus of: "We are staying up". Normally, Pompey fans like to wait until about 4.40pm of the last match in May before they celebrate avoiding relegation. Forty-nine points did the trick in 1998, so the present 51 does nicely, especially since no team has managed that amount after 20 matches over the past five years.

The directors were so excited that they lit celebratory cigars of such potency that they set off the fire alarms in The Chimes bar downstairs. The last time Pompey were in a position as good as this was in 1967. After 20 matches, Pompey were three points clear at the top with 29 – using today's three points for a win, that would have given the team 41 points – five ahead of Birmingham and Blackpool.

The club, as now, had been in a fever of revolution. Unlike Harry Redknapp, who has completely changed the team, the squad of the 1960s had been reduced to 17. Although they lost their lead over the Christmas period, they were thereabouts right until the end of the season, when centre forward Ray Pointer was injured and there was no one to replace him. No wonder Harry was sending out alarms over the injury to striker Vincent Pericard, who limped off during the melée against Walsall last week.

I was reminded of those almost-glory days after a call from my friend, Pete, a West Bromwich Albion fan whom I hadn't spoken to for more than 30 years. First thing he wanted to know was, whatever happened to Ray Hiron? Never mind how's your life? – straight to the essentials.

Now, Hiron was one of the great Pompey stalwarts. He was an ever-present from 1964 to 1975: played 358, scored 117. Born down the road in Fareham, he worked in the dockyard and signed for the club during his lunchbreak. The crowd, with great unoriginality, called him Twiggy because he was tall and, er, thin.

Hiron scored a consolation goal in the fifth round of the FA Cup in 1968 against the great West Bromwich team that included Jeff Astle, Tony Brown and John Talbot. The only way I could get a seat was next to Pete in the West Bromwich end of the ground (D Stand, Row K, Seat 41, Price 7s 6d). When Pompey scored, I was on my feet and cheering – to the bemusement of the surrounding Baggies Brigade. Thank God they were winning because their bemusement might have turned to bovver.

Ray is still around. If you fight your way through the haze of body odour and Brut, you can find him in Portsmouth's Mountbatten Sports Centre, where he quietly sorts out bookings and looks after health and safety.

He has seen Portsmouth only once this season and although he didn't quite say that today's players have it easy, he did remind me that the footballs were so much heavier in his day. He should know. Etched in his memory are two goals – his hundreth against Nottingham Forest at the Milton End, and his first at the Fratton End – both headers.

"My biggest disappointment was that I had to do all the donkey work and was expected to score as well," he said. "Manager George Smith bought in a forward called Bill Atkins towards the end of the season and I scored seven goals in four games. I was looking to the next season when, for some reason, Bill was sold."

Those were the days when the team travelled to away matches by train. Before an FA Cup game against Tottenham Hotspur in 1967 (Gilzean, Greaves, England et al) Ray's car was shunted by a coal van on the way to join the lads at Havant station. No wonder he looked a bit discombobulated during the match, although that might also have been something to do with the fact that he was faced with the combined might of Dave Mackay and Cyril 'Nice one' Knowles.

The lesson Pompey learnt from the one-squad system is that it didn't work. "You have to have a reserve side," Ray said. "Harry understands the system so well with his loans and frees. He's a canny operator, definitely."

More from 'Arry's Bargain Basement. He needs a striker. Will he grab Les Fedinand from Tottenham, or Deon Burton from Derby County? Or could it be Shefki Kuqi from Sheffield Wednesday?

ANORAK'S CORNER
December 7
Reading 0 Portsmouth 0
Crowd: 23,462
Team: Hislop, Ritchie, Taylor, De Zeeuw, Primus, Foxe, Quashie, Robinson, Merson, Todorov, Burchill (Harper).
Substitutes: Kawaguchi, O'Neil, Crowe, Pitt.

Portsmouth, by now seven points clear at the top, were looking for their fifth win in a row, Reading their seventh. The home side created the better chances and looked hungrier. Striker Nicky Forster for Reading was the best player on the pitch with two good chances in the first 30 minutes. Pompey's best chance went to Todorov but he fell over the ball on the edge of the area. Redknapp said: "If I'm being honest, I would have settled for a point beforehand. We've got a million miles to go."

December 14

CUP THAT CHEERS

It's a bit like an Abba revival session in the Portsmouth boardroom. They are all humming along to that telling little ditty:

Money, money, money, Must be sunny, In the rich man's world.

Yesterday, peering at the crowds clutching credit cards as they queued past the terraced houses of Frogmore Road, there must have been much rubbing of hands at the prospect of what must be the biggest cash bonanza in the club's history.

The fans, like sport-loving Assyrians, came down like wolves to buy tickets at £25 a go for the third-round FA Cup tie against Manchester United. They started camping out at 7pm on Thursday and by 8am yesterday there were two one-mile queues. Every taxi firm and bus company has been hired to carry 9,000 fans on the long journey north. The place has gone crazy.

The fans, the players and the management have already raised their eyes to the great Premiership pot of gold as the team gallops away, still seven points clear at the top of the Nationwide League First Division. This game encapsulates the whole glittering business in one afternoon.

This one match is worth £750,000 to the club thanks to Sky

TV and the 45 per cent share of the gate. If it goes to a replay, well, even with Pompey's paltry capacity of 19,000, that means more money, money, money. Maybe a million. Given Harry Redknapp's cheese-paring, that pays the bills for a lot of players.

Just think, only four dismal years ago, as the club headed for administration, the players staged their own wry demonstration against being sold off as a job lot by crayoning their self-valuations on their undershirts.

The result hardly matters. As Peter Storrie, the chief executive, put it: "We have to treat this as a lovely day out. I would rather have this one game than three ordinary rounds at home. If we lose, it won't matter that much because we have to get into the Premiership. That's all that matters. But if we draw, it would be fantastic, and if we win, we would be over the moon."

Encounters between Pompey and Manchester United have been distinctly under the moon. There was an epic at Old Trafford in 1994 in the Coca-Cola Cup, when the might of Giggs, Cantona, Robson and Bruce were held to a 2-2 draw. No Portsmouth fans there that day are in any doubt that they deserved at least one penalty for a foul on Paul Walsh. They lost the replay 1-0.

There was another mighty FA Cup meeting in the 1949-50 season, when Portsmouth, then the power in the land, held United to a 3-3 away draw with goals from such legends as Ike Clarke, Cliff Parker and Harry Ferrier. The replay attracted a frenzy akin to today. It was held on a Wednesday afternoon – this being the era before floodlights – and it seemed the whole of Portsmouth turned out, skipping school and work, claiming sick relatives and bouts of smallpox.

One lad, John Davies, who went on to play for the club, was sacked from his job as an office boy in a solicitor's office because he could not resist the lure of Fratton Park, the theatre of his dreams. In front of nearly 50,000 supporters, Pompey were soundly defeated 3-1. When Pompey met United in the year they were finally relegated from the old Division One, they lost 3-1 at home and 6-1 away. And if you are looking for gloomier omens, take the first time they met; it was 102 years ago come this January 5. Portsmouth lost 3-0.

Still, it's the league that matters and the club secretary has banned all talk of the Cup until the next five league games – all within the space of 18 days – are over. After all, a win away to Stoke City today is more important than a win at Old Trafford.

I put a tenner on Pompey winning the Cup two weeks ago at 100-1, the words of Abba ringing in my ears:

So I must leave, I'll have to go
To Las Vegas or Manchester
And win a fortune in a game
My life will never be the same.

More from 'Arry's Bargain Basement. Deon Burton is back from Derby County after a successful loan period at the start of the season – a snip at £250,000. Matthew Upson, the defender who played a blinder against Pompey in the drab 0-0 draw with Reading, is the latest target. He was on loan from Arsenal and won't come cheap. But, hey, Harry's now got money, money, money.

ANORAK'S CORNER

December 14
Stoke City 1 Portsmouth 1
Scorer: Crowe (74)
Crowd: 13,300
Team: Hislop, Robinson (Crowe), Ritchie (Harper), De Zeeuw, Primus, Foxe, Quashie, Diabate, Merson, Todorov, Burton. Substitutes: Kawaguchi, O'Neil, Burchill.

Stoke dominated the first half and scored in the 33rd minute against a Portsmouth side who did not have one shot on goal in the entire first half. They improved in the second half, putting Stoke under pressure until a pass from Linvoy Primus found substitute Crowe.

December 21
PART OF THE FURNITURE

You used to be able to buy a copy of the football special at Fratton station within minutes of the last kick of the game.

So fast was it off the presses – and this was in the days when papers were put together by grumpy old men and an archaic printing system that used chunks of hot metal – I could catch the 5.28 to Woking and read all about it on the way home. A treat now denied us in these hi-tech days.

At the top of the front page was a caricature sailor. He's still there. If Portsmouth win, he bursts off the page, thumbs up, face wreathed with manic merriment. A defeat is signalled by thumbs down and a grimace of despair. A draw is greeted with a look of such ambiguity even the Mona Lisa would become a fan.

The newspaper character has an alter ego – the Pompey mascot – a jolly chap who capers round the pitch in full matelot's kit, though in recent years he has been overshadowed by a dog and this season by a blue frog. Well, that's showbiz.

Last week, I met the man who was not only the mascot between 1964 and 1973 but who has, for more than 50 years, given all his spare time and passion to the club. Managers (17 of them) and players come and go but Barry 'The Furniture' Harris has been there for ever.

He went to his first game when he was eight: February 23, 1952 against Doncaster Rovers in the FA Cup and Pompey won 4-0. "We were," Barry said, "the Manchester United of the day."

He took to hanging around the ground and was soon helping to tidy up the changing-rooms and sort out the kit. He even chose a job as a self-employed window cleaner so that he could follow the team all over. Let's hope he didn't get his sponges muddled.

A bluff Hampshire lad, now 59, he is a model of discretion about his heroes and mentors. *The Sun* once tried to buy him up – but you'll get no unkind gossip from Barry. He admired the uncompromising George Smith, who enjoyed some success in the Sixties as manager, not least because he hired him as the mascot after he had left the Merchant Navy.

By the Eighties, he was working with the reserves as a physio and came into close contact with the managers. Bobby Campbell was adventurous but reluctant to invest in the defence and he thinks highly of Alan Ball, his successor, who brought in two uncompromising defenders in Micky Kennedy and Noel Blake and won promotion in 1987.

"There were some scallywags in that side. As well as Blake and Kennedy, there was Kevin Dillon and Billy Gilbert. Bally knew how to get the best out of them and keep them under control," he said.

Harris has warm words for Frank Burrows, who steered the club out of the old Fourth Division in 1980. "He brought back the pride in the club and he also got the crowd singing the *Pompey Chimes* again, which had fallen silent for many years."

As for Graham Rix, who had a miserable year until Harry Redknapp took over at the end of last season, Harris said: "I felt sorry for him; he was a nice guy out of his depth."

And Harry? "We have had so many disappointing years, it is hard to believe the way he has turned the club round. It's lovely to see such class as Paul Merson and Matthew Taylor at Fratton Park. They are as good as I've seen."

His favourite players include Jimmy Dickinson, who saw the club through the triumphant years of the Forties to the miseries of the early Sixties, Bobby Kellard, Kennedy – a bit like Merson without the sublime flashes – Andy Awford and Alan Knight, the goalkeeper who played 683 games.

Now, Barry is in his own blue heaven, cooking for the players after away matches. "They eat so much more healthily than they used to," he said. "In George Smith's day, the players would have a steak before a game. Now it's all pasta before and after, though Hayden Foxe does like his shepherd's pie."

More from 'Arry's Bargain Basement. He's finally signed Steve Stone from Aston Villa on a free transfer and has been linked again with Shefki Kuqi of Sheffield Wednesday. Here's some early sales news: buy the gold away strip for the Manchester United game and you'll get £10 off.

ANORAK'S CORNER

December 21
Portsmouth 1 Ipswich 1
Scorer: Todorov (19)
Crowd: 19,130
Team: Hislop, Stone (Harper), Taylor, De Zeeuw, Primus, Foxe, Quashie, Diabate, Merson (O'Neil), Todorov, Burton (Burchill).
Substitutes: Kawaguchi, Ritchie.

The biggest home crowd of the season saw Pompey take the lead when goalkeeper Marshall dropped a centre from Matthew Taylor at the feet of Todorov, for the Bulgarian to score his 12th goal. Ipswich had numerous chances to equalise and grabbed one in the 54th minute when Magilton took a corner on the right and Gaardsoe headed home. This was the game that saw the debut of Merson's winter gloves – and his grumpy chucking off of the captain's arm band when he was substituted in the second half.

December 26
Portsmouth 1 Crystal Palace 1
Scorer: Merson (27)
Crowd: 19,217
Team: Hislop, Crowe (Harper), Taylor, De Zeeuw, Primus, Foxe, Quashie, Diabate (O'Neil), Merson, Todorov, Burton (Pericard). Substitutes: Kawaguchi, Burchill.

Portsmouth took the lead despite struggling to find any kind of form when Taylor ran 60 yards before setting up an easy chance for Merson to score his seventh of the season. Palace equalised almost immediately when the Portsmouth defence cleared a centre only as far as Gray. Hislop denied Palace taking both points with a brilliant save from Akinbiyi.

December 28

KILLER SHAKA

They had that George Best in the directors' box last week and it
made me realise that they have never really gone in for glamour
at Fratton Park. No sex symbols here, thank you. They tried it
with Peter Marinello in the 1970s. He had the looks, but,
unfortunately, not the talent. Alan Biley? With *that* mullet?
Darren Anderton and Neil Webb? Too clean-cut.

There was, of course, George Ley, the defender who won a
nationwide vote among fans for the best-looking player of the
year in the late 1960s, easily beating Bestie, who, at the time,
was the sexiest footballer on the planet. Even the most stalwart
Portsmouth fan had to admit that it was a fix, for although Ley
had a certain B-movie appeal, he was not in the same league.

Now there is Neil S. Hislop, the coolest dude in town.
Amazing what a name can do for a man. Neil Hislop could be a
bit player in *The Office*. Shaka Hislop sounds like a man named
after a Zulu chief, which is just what he is. His Trinidadian
father had obviously decided to keep the options open when he
named him.

Shaka was one of the many summer signings by Harry
Redknapp and his arrival solved a big problem. At the
beginning of last season, the goalkeeping job was given to
Aaron Flahavan, whose career had been blighted by inexplicable
fainting fits. Days before the big kick-off, he died in a car crash.
Pompey scrambled around for a replacement and signed the
unfortunate Yoshi Kawaguchi, who cost a club record £1.8
million and played only a handful of matches before being
dropped. His replacement, the legendary Dave Beasant,
managed remarkably well for a fortysomething but was hardly a
long-term prospect.

Enter Shaka, whose career had taken a dive for the second

time. In 1998, he had been supplanted at Newcastle United by Shay Given when he received a timely call from Redknapp, then manager of West Ham United. He played 132 games for West Ham until November 2001, when he lost his place to David James. Again it was Redknapp who made the call, bringing him south on a free transfer (what else?) eight months later.

At 33, Hislop is tall, languid and athletic. When I watched him in training, he was quick and decisive with a cry of "Shaka's here" as he swooped to gather the ball. So far this season he has conceded fewer goals in the league than Kawaguchi did in his 12 appearances last season – although that does have something to do with the defence, only one of whom has survived from last season.

Between wondering what he should be buying for Christmas – he is married with three daughters – I joked that he has had hardly anything to do all season. He politely pointed out that it was difficult to concentrate when the action was always at the other end of the pitch, but he proved how good he is against Ipswich Town and against Crystal Palace on Boxing Day. In fact, as Portsmouth falter with four draws in their past four games, he is the player of the moment.

He told the supporters' club: "I don't think goalkeepers are as crazy as they used to be," while admitting an admiration for the keeping skills of the eccentric Bruce Grobelaar. "When you think about it, there are ten outfield players whose only job is to blast the ball as hard as they past me and I have to get any part of my body in the way to stop it. Now that doesn't make much sense. Every goalkeeping mistake is scrutinised and highlighted a lot more. It is an unforgiving position. You are remembered more for your mistakes than for your saves."

There is a lot more to Shaka than goalkeeping. Raised in Trinidad – his school pals were Dwight Yorke and Brian Lara – he studied mechanical engineering at an American university and turned to football only after he was spotted by a Reading scout playing in a friendly match for Baltimore Blasts. In 1992, he signed for the Berkshire club.

On the website for the Trinidad national team, Shaka talks about trying to keep up with the workings of football at boardroom level. "Football is going through a very interesting transition and the amount of money involved is huge," he says. "I'm a student of that; it keeps my mind active and alive."

That might explain why he was one of the first players to take advantage the Bosman transfer when he made his move from Newcastle to West Ham and his affinity with Redknapp, another man who understands the transfer system. Shaka enthuses about the down-to-earth personality of his manager and his ability to engender enthusiasm among the players. The training session I watched was characterised as much by laughter as hard work, though that might change as the pressure at the top grows.

Luckily, Shaka's there.

More from 'Arry's Bargain Basement. The big disappointment is the probable departure of Mark Burchill, a fans' favourite who never really figured in Harry's plans. He will make the club a big profit on the £600,000 that Graham Rix paid for him last season.

ANORAK'S CORNER

December 28
Nottingham Forest 1 Portsmouth 2
Scorers: Taylor (56), Pericard (87)
Crowd: 28,165
Team: Hislop, Harper (Crowe), Taylor, De Zeeuw, Primus, Foxe, Quashie, Diabate, O'Neil, Todorov, Burton (Pericard).
Substitutes: Kawaguchi, Robinson, Burchill.

Portsmouth outplayed Forest despite the absence of the injured Merson and Stone, but did not take the lead until a thunderous

20-foot left-foot drive from Taylor in the 56th minute. Substitute Pericard scored a tap-in after goalkeeper Ward fumbled Crowe's shot. Forest scored a consolation goal in stoppage time.

January 1
Watford 2 Portsmouth 2
Scorers: Crowe (54), Harper (58)
Crowd: 15,048
Team: Hislop, Harper, Taylor, De Zeeuw (Crowe), Primus, Foxe, Quashie, Diabate, O'Neil, Todorov (Merson), Burton (Pericard). Substitutes: Kawaguchi, Stone.

Arjan De Zeeuw limped off with a knee ligament injury after only five minutes as Portsmouth were forced to a draw by a surprisingly effective opposition. Watford dominated after the break with Pennant particularly effective on the right. It was his cross that led to Hyde scoring. Burton hit back three minutes later and Harper with a superb curling shot put Portsmouth ahead. Watford deservedly equalised with ten minutes to go with a Cox header.

CHAPTER 6

JANUARY

January 4
HARRY'S GAME

All tics, twitches and non-stop talk, ear clamped to his mobile, Harry Redknapp arrives at Portsmouth's training ground and promptly adjourns to the changing room for 40 minutes. "He'll be doing a deal," the man from Quay Radio said.

It has been by doing deals that Redknapp has utterly transformed Portsmouth. That and the combined footballing wisdom of himself and Jim Smith, the assistant manager. After years of last-ditch scrapes from relegation, chaotic management, near-bankruptcy and early exits from the FA Cup at the hands of teams such as Leyton Orient, the future is looking as golden as the team's away strip.

Portsmouth are five points clear at the top of the Nationwide League First Division and today it's Manchester United at Old Trafford in the third round of the Cup, the biggest crowd that Portsmouth have played in front of since 1952 and a million in the bank, win or lose.

"I'd be daft to forecast a win," Redknapp said, "but it's a

perfect draw for us. It's a lovely day out and a great opportunity to play against the best."

What a difference a year makes. Last Christmas, he had been lampooned by the local paper for sloping off on a Caribbean holiday while the club flirted with relegation. He was director of football and loathing it.

"It was the worst year of my life," he said. "I don't know why I took the job but I was persuaded by Milan Mandaric, the chairman. I took it even though my strengths are not being an office worker. I need to get out on the training ground and do what I enjoy: being involved with players, bringing players in, making decisions on who plays. I found I was not a lot of use."

Nor was he greeted as a saviour when he replaced Graham Rix for the fag-end of the season. Many thought he would do well to last the average eight months that managers enjoy under Mandaric's impatient reign. The fans hated him selling Peter Crouch, the player of the year, and they rated his replacement, Svetoslav Todorov, a no-hoper. In the event, Todorov has already scored 12 goals and Crouch earned the club a handy £3.5 million profit.

Now, ten months later, the revolution roars on and every fan in the 35 coachloads heading north this morning will be singing a chorus of that Fratton End favourite that ends with a cheery *"Harry is our King"*, and, no doubt, rehearsing a ribald little ditty involving Posh, Becks and Paul Merson. Don't ask.

Did he really think it would be as good as this? "No, nowhere near. I felt there was something sick about the club. Long before I got involved, it seemed to me, from talking to people like Ted MacDougall, who was a coach here, that this was one of the clubs where there was something wrong, which was impossible to sort out. The support is fantastic, but it just seemed that whoever came here, it wouldn't make any difference.

"I thought, 'This isn't going to be easy'. I didn't know how far we'd go, but I knew we had to bring a new squad in. There were lots of players around the place who had no interest in the football. I don't know where they had even come from and why they were there. The Rundonjas (Mladen Rundonja, from Slovenia, who never made a start) and the Panopouloses (Mihailis Panopoulos, from Greece, signed by Alan Ball), all these people. Who were they?"

Like all managers, Redknapp brought in his own players. The supporters looked on in amazement as the list grew. At the last count, it was 16 in (loans and transfers) and 18 out. Only Nigel Quashie, Gary O'Neil and Linvoy Primus have survived from last year.

"I had no doubts," Redknapp said. "This is what I've spent my life doing. I did it at Bournemouth, when I took them into the First Division picking up people on free transfers (and beating Manchester United in the Cup on the way) and when I took over West Ham, which was a yo-yo side."

Does he resent the inevitable jibe that he's just a wheeler-dealer? "I do, yes, because I really don't want to be. I'd like to take over a team where you don't have to do that." But immediately contradicting himself: "But I'm always looking for new players. If you see someone who can improve your side slightly, then you've got to do it.

"When I was at West Ham, I bought Michael Hughes from Strasbourg. Then Eyal Berkovic came available in the same position, so I let Hughesy go for £1.5 million and brought Berkovic in for the same.

"But I would rather not be on the phone all the time. If I was at Man United or if I was Arsene Wenger, I wouldn't have to. If I was Micky Adams at Leicester with his squad, I wouldn't need to bring a player in."

The local press corps has come to admire his sheer hard work. "If you ask him the name of some reserve player for Colchester, he'll know everything about him," one said. "He's always at a game, he's always making inquiries, checking, phoning."

"I'm out most nights if there is a game on because there are players out there if you look hard enough," Redknapp said. "I have been to reserve games at Spurs, Brentford and Arsenal in the last week. There are some Arsenal players I wouldn't hesitate to bring in – but only on a loan.

"We got Middlesbrough to pay most of Gianluca Festa's wages and we did a deal over Paul Merson. We pay what we can afford."

Merson, Redknapp's most publicised signing, has become the club's talisman, with almost as much influence off the pitch as on it. "I like people who play like that, who can turn a game with one pass," Redknapp said. "When I signed (Paolo) Di Canio for the second time, people said I was mad and they said the same about Merson because he has a lot of baggage, but he's a fantastic footballer who the players love. I love having someone like that in my team.

"Matthew Taylor, Linvoy Primus, Todorov... they've all done well, every one of them. Take Arjan De Zeeuw, he's a fantastic person." Sadly for Portsmouth, De Zeeuw will not be playing today, leaving the defence to the redoubtable Hayden Foxe and Harry's latest, last-minute signing, Stathis Tavlaridis, from Arsenal – a reward for all those evenings watching reserve games.

"What we don't want to do is go up there and get a real hammering," Redknapp said. "We mustn't show fear or be afraid to tackle Beckham. We must compete, get stuck in and close down the game. Alex Ferguson will warn them against playing the underdogs, but he's lucky, he's got competition for places with players fighting for their lives to keep out the Ferdinands and Beckhams."

Pure Redknapp.

He twitches through the curtains of the club house and peers out at his 'good lads' playing five-a-side under the gaze of Jim Smith.

"We've only got 11 players, it's frightening. We've got no squad here, no cover for injuries. Linvoy Primus has a hernia, Merson can only play with injections, only two centre halves and another has the flu."

Nonetheless the players are in high spirits, laughing and joking as they come off the training pitch.

What's his secret weapon for today's match? There isn't one. "I try to keep them relaxed and keep the pressure off. I don't have long meetings in the hotel before the game, I just try to create a good atmosphere."

Then the phone goes and Harry's off, taking every game as it comes and every phone call as it's made.

ANORAK'S CORNER

January 4
FA Cup
Manchester United 4 Portsmouth 1
Scorer: Stone (39)
Crowd: 67,222
Team: Hislop, Harper, Taylor, Tavlaridis, Primus, Foxe, Quashie, Diabate (O'Neil), Merson (Burton), Todorov, Stone (Pericard).
Substitutes: Kawaguchi, Crowe.

It all looked so easy for United. One up after four minutes, thanks to a Nistelrooy penalty after he had been fouled by Primus, and two down after 17, thanks to a devastating Beckham free kick. United were strolling it until a free kick from Taylor and a header on from Foxe found Stone four yards out and happy to score. Portsmouth played well in the second half and Quashie, sent clear by substitute O'Neil, shot over the bar with only the goalkeeper to beat. United rallied, Nistelrooy was fouled again, this time by Foxe, and scored

from the spot, and Scholes scored in the dying seconds. But it was a
great day out.

January 11
STONE'S CERTAINTY

So we're sitting on a Virgin train to Manchester. We have all
been up since well before dawn and pretty soon, as we edge past
the end of platform 14, the conversation turns to football. Since
the entire train is filled with supporters in blue and white
heading for the cup tie with Manchester United it's hardly likely
to turn to something trivial like the war in Iraq. We are resigned
to Portsmouth losing, though there is a quick fantasy about
Linvoy Primus, the stalwart defender, scoring a hat trick, and
settle for a 4-1 defeat.

And so it came to pass. One of the few players who really
impressed, who didn't look either terrified or out of sorts in the
first half, was Steve Stone. He scored the goal and worked
tirelessly. Well, he has done it all before, accumulating nine
England caps in the process.

Nonetheless, for a successful player he has had a difficult year,
one which offers a glimpse into the vagaries and insecurities of
modern football, far from the gilded world of the Beckhams and
Zolas.

Stone, 31, had to be rescued by Harry Redknapp from the
purgatory of rejection at Aston Villa, where he fell out of favour
with manager Graham Taylor and did not make a start for six
months. A mere three years previously, he had been bought by
the club from Notts Forest for more than £5 million.
Considering that Paul Merson suffered a similar fate, it is no
wonder that they chant: *'There's only one Graham Taylor'* at
Fratton Park. Stone said: "I sat around at Villa and hated it.

"It's odd working and training through the week but having to do nothing on Saturday. You just don't know what to do with yourself. It is quite nice to spend time with the family every now and then, but, after a while, being on the bench or not playing at all gets depressing. After all, what I do is play football and if I can't, it all gets very frustrating.

"I suppose I can understand it; there's a new manager with new ideas and I have no doubt he had to get to grips with the wage bill.

"Now, it's just nice to be playing again."

On top of the insecurity, there is the have-boots-will-travel lifestyle. He had already despatched his wife and four girls from the Midlands to their home city of Newcastle, so that the 14-year-old could concentrate on her GCSEs. Now he commutes by air once or twice a week from Southampton to the north-east and lives in the local Marriot hotel – all very functional but no place like home.

"It's all right," he said. "I tuck myself up in my room out of the cold and keep myself to myself. I keep hearing about all these new players that Harry is bringing in and I think they are all staying in the hotel. The place is so full of foreigners that I think I'm the only Englishman here."

The consolation for his dislocated existence is that he is playing first-team football again and possibly playing it in the Premiership again next season. "I was impressed with the talent at the club when I was here on loan in October, but the side is a long way from having the kind of quality needed to survive if they go up. The standard will have to improve and we'll need to add a lot of players to our squad. As we learned from the United game, we need a squad big enough to cope with injuries and sharp enough to cope with players who are in the class of Van Nistelrooy."

Even for veterans, there are new tricks to learn and Stone is

enjoying the double-act master classes of Harry 'n' Jim –
Redknapp and Smith.

"I like watching them sorting things out. I wish I had been
there at the beginning of the season when they had just got
together for the first time and were working out their routine.
Now they have got it off it a tee, bouncing ideas off each other.

"It can be very lonely being a manager but they are a great
team who get on well with each other, help each other and are
always happy to talk to the players."

**More from 'Arry's Bargain Basement. He's been busy.
Finnish defender Markus Heikkinen is on a three-month
loan from HJK Helsinki, a couple of Danes have been on
trial, and Yakubu Aiyegbeni of Maccabi Haifa has been
signed for the rest of the season with the option, according
to one newspaper, of buying him for £4million plus. No
wonder Stone thought he was in a foreign country.**

ANORAK'S CORNER

January 11
Portsmouth 1 Sheffield United 2
Scorer: O'Neil (78)
Crowd: 18,882
Team: Hislop, Stone (Harper), Festa (Tavlaridis), Primus, Foxe,
Taylor, O'Neil, Quashie, Merson, Todorov (Burton), Pericard.
Substitutes: Kawaguchi, Diabate.

*United arrived cheered by their 2-1 Worthington Cup semi-final
first-leg win over Liverpool, but Portsmouth started the better with
Taylor and Foxe both wasting chances inside the first ten minutes.
Sheffield scored first when Ndlovu played a neat one-two with
Tonge to send a deflected shot past Hislop from 10 yards. Merson
almost equalised in the 75th minute, but it was O'Neil who latched
on to a pass from Tavlaridis to chip home from six yards.
Unfortunately, Brown seized on a mistake by Foxe for the winner.*

Merson was booed by a small, impatient, stupid section of the crowd.

January 18
KNICKERS FOR JASON

Had you stepped into the intimate world of Classique Lingerie in Portsmouth on Thursday with your eye on a pair of big knickers and a thong in your heart, you would have been rocked by the roar of the *Pompey Chimes* echoing around the boutique.

The music is usually more refined, but Heather Emery, the owner, had just popped down to the Portsmouth club shop and bought *The Season So Far* on DVD for her son and couldn't wait until she got home. She's more than just a supporter, she is also on the lookout to promote her shop. What better than combining business with passion and sponsoring a player?

So there in the programme, alongside the smiling face of Jason Crowe, the sprightly wing back, is the logo of Classique Lingerie. Why Jason? He was the only one left when they applied to sponsor a player last season. For £400 (plus VAT) the sponsor pays for the kit, gets their name in the programme, enjoys hospitality in the VIP suite two games a season, and eats, drinks and rubs shoulders with Fratton celebs. All the player of choice has to do is turn up once a season to sign a shirt and have his picture taken shaking hands.

Harry Redknapp, the manager, also has a sponsor, the Bluebell Nursing Home in Southsea. After Monday's defeat against Sheffield United, he was said to be utterly devastated so he might be tempted to borrow a room for a lie-down. Perhaps he will take Paul Merson with him. He is also pretty fed up.

Poor Merse was got at during the game by impatient fans and said: "It was disappointing because I have never been booed at any time in my career. I tried to play a few passes that didn't come off, but if the fans want me to, I can play five-yard balls all day."

It's certainly true that Merson has been off the pace since a Sheffield Wednesday player stamped on his ankle in November. Until then, he had been like Legolas, the archer in *The Lord of the Rings*, shooting passes like arrows around the ground, totally destroying the opposition. Even if he has lost some of that braggadocio, he is still the most intelligent player on the pitch.

Shocking, really, how fickle the crowd can be, but then the side has won only one game in the past eight. Some fans are more tolerant, not least Merson's own sponsor, Grant Cameron, the managing director of Concurrent Design Group, which produces computer-aided designs for engineering firms. It will take more than a few duff games to dampen his enthusiasm for the player.

Grant, a supporter for 27 years, said: "I think he slipped a bit when he started wearing those gloves. He is still a class player and he was magic for the first 20 games. He was the one who gave us the winning touch."

For Concurrent, there is a marketing bonus. "It is a small investment but we get our name in the programme and Merson is a good name to be linked with," Grant said. It's irresistible really, buying into a little touch of stardust.

Giuseppe Mascia is the owner of the Pizza House Restaurant and sponsors Vincent Pericard, the French-born, Italian-speaking striker on loan from Juventus. Signor Mascia, a voluble Sardinian whose English is as impenetrable as it was 26 years ago when he warmed his first bowl of pasta in Portsmouth, is unashamedly star-struck.

"The chairman, Milan Mandaric, is a good friend of mine," he said. "He is often coming in here, such a kind man, so committed to the club. He is unique. He is always inviting me to the directors' box. He asked me to sponsor Vincent because we speak Italian and he thought it would be nice for him..

"He's a nice boy. I give him free drinks – only soft ones, of course – and deliver pizza and pasta to his flat. I like giving him treats like coffees, Christmas cake and ice-cream."

Back in the silky environs of Classique Lingerie, Heather Emery is rather more pragmatic. She has yet to meet her trophy player and he certainly hasn't been in her shop, but being part of the scene has done wonders for her networking with local businesses and lots of the women at the club have bought her gear.

Even the supporters' club sponsors a player and last year auctioned off Dave Beasant's gear to raise funds. One fanatic even paid good money for his socks. But usually they are discerning types and talk on Monday wasn't so much that Merson had played badly but that Harry had used the wrong formation and should give Merse a rest. Anyone got the number for the Bluebell Nursing Home?

More from 'Arry's Bargain Basement. After last week's frenzy, in which three new players were signed on loan, Yakubu Aiyegbeni, the Nigeria striker, is on the bench today against Brighton and Hove Albion. He is already being hailed as an "exciting new signing" but has yet to kick a ball.

ANORAK'S CORNER

January 18
Brighton 1 Portsmouth 1
Scorer: Todorov (64)
Crowd: 6,848
Team: Hislop, Stone (Harper), Taylor, Tavlaridis (Crowe), Primus, Foxe, Quashie, Diabate, Merson, Todorov, Pericard (Aiyegbeni). Substitutes: Kawaguchi, Burton.

Portsmouth were held to their fourth draw in six games by bottom-placed Brighton, who were by no means overawed. Todorov had appeals for a penalty turned down and Quashie – against the run of play – had two fine shots saved on either side of the interval. Brighton went ahead with a superbly taken goal by Zamora and that galvanized Portsmouth into action. New Nigerian striker Yakubu Aiyegbeni came on and almost scored with his first touch. Then Todorov picked up a Quashie pass to strike his 13th goal of the season.

January 25
HARRY'S WIT AND WISDOM

The second round of the FA Cup saw Portsmouth take a break. Redknapp jetted off to Barbados for sun and a pina colada or three.

To while away the time, *True Blue*, the supporters' club magazine, edited by Andy Dobbs, published some verbal highlights from the great man. Including this priceless moment.

The internet is a wonderful thing. Not only can you get a cheap flight, but you can also read some great pearls of wisdom from some of the great thinkers around the world, like our very own Harry. Take a recent video clip where Harry was giving a TV interview. Here is the transcript:

Harry is giving a pre-match interview on the sidelines at Portsmouth's training ground. Two reserve players are having a kickabout in the background.

Redknapp (in mid-sentence): "Gianluca Festa's having a scan today and we're hoping it's not as serious as it looks, Arjan De Zeeuw's done a groin..."

At this point, a stray ball hits Harry hard on his back. Redknapp (shouting and glaring at offending player): "Why the **** have you kicked that over here? What? What? You tried to kick it in the goal and you hit me? Got some ****ing brains, ain't you?"

Reporter (desperately trying to save interview while a clearly furious Redknapp goes through repertoire of facial tics and Paddington Bear hard stares at the unfortunate player): "Sorry Harry, just a last word on Wolves... it's a big game, a game at Molineux, a big crowd, it's a big match for you."

*Redknapp: "Yeah, it's a big match." (One last stern look at offending player.) "No wonder he's in the ****ing reserves."*

MORE PEARLS...

On his former West Ham striker: "John Hartson's got more previous than Jack the Ripper."

On the ignoble art of 'simulation'! "Abou retaliated but the fellow went down as if he was dead, and then started rolling around."

On his relationship as Portsmouth's Director of Football with the club's then manager: "I shall not be interfering with Graham Rix."

On tactics: "I sorted out the team formation last night lying in bed with the wife. When your husband's as ugly as me, you'd only want to talk football in bed."

On a training-ground scrap between Alvin Martin and Matthew Rush: "I've seen better fights at a wedding."

On Somassi Abou: "He don't speak the English too good."

On a striker he subsequently signed, who went on to score just two goals for West Ham: "I look at Arsenal's bench and they have Davor Suker sitting there. The man's a legend and would score goals by the bucketload whoever he played for."

On West Ham's UEFA Cup chances: "Where are we in relation to Europe? Not too far from Dover."

On a spurned chance against Chelsea: "Joe Cole missed an open goal that my ****ing missus could have scored."

On his playing career: "Even when we had Moore, Hurst and Peters, West Ham's average finish was about 17th. Which just shows how crap the other eight of us were."

On Paolo Di Canio's one-fingered gesture to Aston Villa fans: "From a still picture, how does anybody know what Di Canio was doing? He might have been signalling to a team-mate about a tactic from a corner. He might have been gesturing a tactical change. He could have been showing that the score was 1-0."

On signing good-looking Portuguese winger, Dani, he told reporters: "My missus fancies him. Even I don't know whether to play him or **** him."

BLAME IT ON RIO

One of Harry's finest hours was Rio Ferdinand's protracted transfer to Leeds United. On April 28 2000, Harry told *The London Evening Standard*: "David O'Leary did enquire about Rio, but we're not interested in selling any of our young stars. We want to go forward as a club and selling Rio now would be a backward step."

On April 29, Harry told *The Sun*: "David O'Leary has £30 million to spend in the summer and he wants to give me £10 million for Rio Ferdinand. But the day we sell Rio and our other young players is the day when this club starts to die."

On August 12, Harry told Sky Sports: "The chairman of Leeds is trying to manipulate a deal. It's unsettling for Rio and for this club, and I'm fed up. I know what's been going on. If Barcelona knock on the door, we've got real problems because I couldn't say, 'No' to the boy. But why should we sell him to Leeds? He's better off here."

On November 25, Harry told *The Standard*: "We don't want to be seen as a selling club. Rio is going nowhere."

On November 26, Rio Ferdinand joined Leeds United.

FOREIGN BODIES

Though his aim seems to have improved since joining Portsmouth, Harry never seemed to have much luck when signing foreign types. This, our hero once explained, was because he couldn't bond with them as well as he did with domestic players.

"With the foreigners, it's more difficult," he said. "Most of them don't even bother with the golf, they don't want to go racing. They don't even drink."

Many rate Harry's greatest deal as the £1m he paid for Marco Boogers, the Dutch caravan-dweller whose sole start for the club ended after 15 minutes when he was sent off for attempting to cut Manchester United's Gary Neville in half. Harry later sagely observed: "You can't get ****-all for a million nowadays."

Others claim his best brush with foreigners was a West Ham trial match against Barnet in 1993, arranged so Harry could run the rule over an exciting Russian prospect. "Andrei Shevchenko didn't pull up any trees," he explained to the press the next day before sending the future Dynamo Kiev and AC Milan superstar on his way.

When explaining Samassi Abou's absence one day: "The lad went home to the Ivory Coast and got a bit of food poisoning. He must have eaten a dodgy missionary or something."

CHAPTER 7

FEBRUARY

February 1

YAK THE LAD

Remember Blackie Gray? I thought not. What about Roy Race, aka Roy of the Rovers? Of course, you remember him, after all, he has been Melchester Rovers' leading goalscorer since 1955. The unfair truth is that strikers grab the headlines while the steadfast midfield players such as Blackie fade into obscurity. No wonder the football talk on the south coast has been dominated by one man. No, not James Beattie, of S**th*mpt*n, but Yakubu Aiyegbeni (or is it Aiyegbeni Yakubu, no one seems too sure), the Nigerian international, and, needless to say, he is a forward.

Harry Redknapp has put £200,000 down for him with an option to pay another £4 million when the club is promoted (sorry, if). Such is the excitement that a dedicated 300 fans turned out this week to watch the new man score once in a reserve game against Barnet. The scepticism of the true Pompey fan is being sorely challenged by the optimistic hope that Yakubu might be something special. He has yet to complete a game but he is already being hailed as the man to rekindle the promotion drive when he makes his home debut against Grimsby Town today.

At the risk of irritating Harry "Blip, what blip?" Redknapp, Pompey have won only one game in the past nine and need a fillip. As one member of the supporters' group, the Pompey Anoraks, emailed: "Leicester are only two points behind now. Funnily enough, I feel calmer – it seems like the real world. If we don't make it to the play-offs, I'll feel completely normal."

That's the problem with being a Portsmouth fan, it imbues you with a sense of scepticism that verges on the pathological. Take Andy Dobbs, a supporter for 27 years and editor of *True Blue*, the supporters' club magazine. He has to tread the line between his passion for the club and the need to dish out the occasional brickbat. In the latest edition, words of praise for the chairman are tempered with brisk criticism of some players and management for not attending the supporters' Christmas party.

Dobbs started working on the magazine in 1989 when it was six photocopied pages of A4 stapled together. He overcame the hostility of his wife to all things football to become the editor four years ago. For him, the conjunction of the words 'Portsmouth', 'false' and 'dawn' is a familiar refrain, particularly when it comes to new strikers.

He runs through a mournful list of has-beens and never-would-have-beens: "Lee Mills cost £1.5 million and Rory Allen £1 million but neither of them really wanted to be here. They just weren't interested. I used to like David Kemp in the late Seventies (he scored 32 goals in 64 games) but he was transferred.

"Colin Garwood did even better (34 goals in 62 games) and was moved on. Mark Hateley scored 22 goals in 1983 and was sold for £1 million. We were always a selling club. We either bought badly or sold anyone with talent."

When it comes to the ultimate letdown, everyone thinks of

Peter Marinello, who cost a massive £100,000 in 1973. The poor lad was hailed as the new George Best and looked like a glam-rock star with his long hair and beatific looks. Unfortunately, he played like a glam-rock star.

As for Yakubu, the 20-year-old helped Maccabi Haifa to become the first club from Israel to feature in the Champions League, scoring in the club's 3-0 win against Manchester United. Let's hope he isn't suckered into the publicity trap that ensnared the young Marinello and let's hope that he hits it off with Harry.

More from 'Arry's Bargain Basement. At last, after six months, he has signed Tim Sherwood from Tottenham Hotspur for £200,000. I reckon that's 19 new players on loans and transfers since he took over. For the next 19, he could adopt a money-raising idea from the Eighties: which Portsmouth player was sponsored by Roy of the Rovers? Answer next week.

ANORAK'S CORNER

February 1
Portsmouth 3 Grimsby 0
Scorers: Aiyegbeni (4), og (75), Quashie (90)
Crowd: 19,428
Team: Hislop, Harper (Crowe), Taylor, Tavlaridis, Primus, Foxe (Diabate), Quashie, Sherwood, Merson, Todorov, Aiyegbeni (Pericard).
Substitutes: Kawaguchi, Burton.

Yakubu Aiyegbeni scored four minutes into his home debut with an electrifying burst, which saw him cut in behind the Grimsby defence. The 20-year-old missed a second chance 10 minutes later. Pompey dominated: Merson nearly scored with a free kick and Tim Sherwood almost celebrated his debut when his shot was deflected. A Taylor cross was deflected into the goal by a Grimsby defender, and, in injury time, Quashie sealed the win when he ran on to a fabulous through-ball from Merson. "A 6-0 victory wrapped in a 3-0 scoreline," said The Times.

February 8
LET'S HEAR IT FOR THE LADS...

There's a revolution sweeping Fratton Park. No, not the football, the music. For the second time this season, the club has won – wait for it – the coveted Stadium Announcer of the Month Award. What's more, in the announcers' league, Pompey are ahead of Manchester United, Liverpool and S**th*mpt*n.

The proud winner is Steve Pearson, cousin of the more famous Stuart, who has qualified for his supernova-dom by the choice of records he plays at each game. He is sent a collection of sounds by an enterprising outfit called Upshot Communications and it awards him points for the number of records played. Even a mention in a newspaper is worth a point – so here's another one, Steve.

His pièce de résistance is to play an appropriate record after one of the lads scores. So if Paul Merson cracks one in, prepare for a celebratory blast of *Rollin'*, by Limp Bizkit. Unfortunately, these inter mezzi are somewhat wasted on the Fratton faithful, where the loudspeaker system is a bit like listening to Björk on speed under an ice floe. Steve, 38, didn't really want to be a DJ. He wanted to be a footballer like Stuart and like his father, who played for Norwich City in the 1940s and 50s. He said: "It was my dream – I was a left full back – but despite signing schoolboy forms in 1978 when Frank Burrows was manager, I never made it.

"Yes, I was upset, but I did get my coaching badge and then went for the next best, which is music. After all, pop stars and football stars are part of the same thing." After a spell on local radio, he got the call to work for the club as announcer and musicologist. "Harry Redknapp and Jim Smith asked me to mix a few tapes for them," he said. "They are both on the road a lot and like easy listening. Harry is very keen on big-band music. He loves Shirley Bassey (*Big Spender* is presumably high on his list), Tom Jones, Dean Martin, and I think Tommy Steele got in there somewhere.

"Jim is also keen on Dean Martin, but likes Coldplay, REM and Foreigner." Steve asked the players what records they wanted to help them celebrate when they scored. Before he opted for Limp Bizkit, Paul Merson chose *Wild Thing*, by the Troggs, though, given Super Paul's benign influence on the team, on field and off, Steve reckons *Starmaker*, by Kids From Fame, might be more appropriate.

Gianluca Festa, who is unlikely ever to score, opted for *Uncle Fester*, the theme from The Addams Family; Deon Burton chose *Who Let the Dogs Out?* by the Baha Men; and Vincent Pericard went for *Nu Flow* by Big Brovaz. Kevin Harper, who has enjoyed a renaissance in recent weeks, went for *Hot in Here* by Nelly. Svetoslav Todorov, the leading goalscorer, couldn't make up his mind, so some of the team chose *Insane in the Brain* by Cypress Hill for him, because "the players think he's nuts".

Now Steve has to find a song for Yakubu Aiyegbeni, the latest addition to the Tune Army. Given his electric turn of pace, contenders are Bruce Springsteen's *Born to Run*, *Speedy Gonzales* by Pat Boone (one for the older fan), and *Greased Lightning* by John Travolta.

How about *Long Distance Runaround* by Yes?

"I wanted to jazz-up the music that had been played before, during and after the game," Pearson said. He persuaded the club to replace the lugubrious *Thus Sprach Zarathustra*, which used to open proceedings, with a musical build-up that starts with *Carnival De Paris* by Dario G, segues into the overture from

Prokofiev's *Swan Lake* and climaxes with Robbie Williams's *Let Me Entertain You.*

He also chooses something to cheer the crowd on its way. Last week, after disposing of Grimsby Town, it was left to KC and the Sunshine Band with *That's The Way (I Like It)*. And he has been magnanimous in defeat.

After the debacle against Leicester City in November, he played *Don't Look Back In Anger*, the Oasis classic.

More from 'Arry's Bargain Basement. There is no more. Not a loan, not a trial, nothing. In a shock announcement Redknapp has promised: "That'll do, we won't be getting any more players." But he did keep the door ajar by adding: "Unless we have a disaster with injuries."

If they have any cash to spare, the club should buy a new loudspeaker system. As Harry's favourite, Shirley Bassey, entreats: "I, who hear nothing, implore you…"

No one remembered which player was sponsored by Roy of the Rovers in the Eighties. It was the superbly-coiffured Alan Biley, who scored 51 goals in 105 appearances.

ANORAK'S CORNER

February 8
Portsmouth 6 Derby 2
Scorers: Merson (3), Aiyegbeni (17, 80), Taylor (22), Todorov (73, 85).
Crowd: 19,503
Team: Hislop, Harper, Taylor, Tavlaridis (Heikkinen), Primus, Foxe, Quashie (Diabate), Sherwood, Merson, Todorov, Aiyegbeni.
Substitutes: Kawaguchi, Pericard, Burton.

Aiyegbeni and Todorov both scored twice as Pompey crushed Derby. They were 3-0 up in 20 minutes with goals from Merson, Yakubu and Taylor.

Derby fought back in the second half with Morris and Kinkladze

*scoring to make it 3-2 with 23 minutes to go. Todorov restored
Portsmouth's two-goal lead on 73 minutes with a neat finish from
Aiyegbeni's pass before the pair combined ten minutes later for the
Nigerian to race through the defence to score a fifth. Todorov scored
off a rebound of his shot from close quarters, hitting the ball into
the roof of the net. What added piquance to it all was not just Derby
manager John Gregory being banished from the touchline for his
unseemly temper but the realisation that he had tried to sign Yakubu
before the season but had failed to get a work permit.*

February 15
A DAY TO REMEMBER

When John Phillips trotted out on to the pitch for his first home
game at Fratton Park, he fulfilled his greatest ambition. He had
been a fan as a boy – now he was playing for his beloved
Portsmouth. It was 1956, he was 18 and on a tenner a game
with a £2 bonus for a win. It all went according to the script. In
front of a crowd of 30,513, Pompey beat Arsenal 5-2 and the
young left half picked up his extra £2.

The Portsmouth team he played for were in slow decline after
the great post-war years when they dominated English football.
Nonetheless, Phillips played alongside Duggie Reid, Peter
Harris and Jimmy Dickinson who, with Jack Froggatt and
Jimmy Scoular, had been among the constellation of greats who
had won the championship two years running.

In an eerie counterpoint to this season's success, seven players
from that era have recently died: Reid and Harris, Ernie Butler,
Ike Clarke, Harry Ferrier, and Albert Mundy. And last week the
Pompey crowd paid silent tribute to Phil Rookes, who died at
the age of 83.

Few of the crowd would have seen him play and it could have
meant little personally to the players who stood heads bowed in

the centre circle, none of whom has local loyalties and only three or four of whom have been with the club for more than six months. But clubs are defined as much by their history as by the present. Players, managers and owners come and go, and the glories and disappointments of the past vie with an eternal optimism.

Take next Monday's game with second-placed Leicester City. It could decide the Nationwide League First Division, but it jangles an old nerve. In 1949, to the horror of fans such as the 11-year-old John Phillips, the best Portsmouth team assembled crashed 3-1 to Leicester, then of the Second Division, in the FA Cup semi-final and fluffed their chance of the Double. Phillips prefers to dwell on the previous round, in which Pompey beat Derby County 2-1 in front of a suffocating crowd of 51,385.

"We were packed in like sardines," he recalled. "But we were used to 40,000-plus crowds. The atmosphere was always great. I used to play football in the morning, race home, take off my boots and go to the game in my football gear. I was only about 4ft 6in so I would hang on the stanchions of the North Stand so that I could see.

"They were really wonderful days because the game was so open with the W formation, not like the midfield now where everything seems to converge in the middle. You can't really compare the teams. Peter Harris, who scored 193 goals in 479 appearances, was so fast, there was a real buzz when he ran on to a through-ball. This new chap, Yakubu, has that same quality. You feel that something is going to happen and that's what crowds have always liked."

Managers are easier to compare. Come what may, Harry Redknapp will be remembered for conjuring up one of the club's most exciting seasons. Phillips played under Freddie Cox, who is still remembered as the club's most disastrous occupant of that hot seat.

"He wanted to impose a new system," Phillips said. "It might have been revolutionary, perhaps even a bit like the way they play today, but what he did was crazy. He dismantled a hell of a good side because he wouldn't face up to the old guard, and, instead, brought in Third Division players and youngsters. He thought he could impose his will on them."

Under Cox, Pompey plummeted from the old First Division to Third in three seasons.

"It was awful, so depressing," Phillips said. "I was put on the transfer list at a stupid price, my contract ran out, and, because I had no money, I left and played non-league football. We were football slaves then."

Now Phillips, 65, pores over his collection of Pompey memorabilia and takes pleasure in the club's renaissance. "That Matthew Taylor is good and the way Todorov ran the length of the pitch against Derby to lay on a goal was brilliant. I've liked the look of Hayden Foxe and Steve Stone.

"But they do seem to lose their way in the second half. When Derby came back to 3-2 last week, I thought, 'Uh-oh, here we go again'. It reminded me of a game against Huddersfield in 1959, the relegation year. We were 3-0 up but somehow we managed to lose 6-3."

More from 'Arry's Bargain Basement. He said it was all over. It isn't quite. Last week, it was: "No more new players." This week, he signed Sasa Ilic as reserve goalkeeper. By my reckoning, that makes it two new players a month since he took over.

ANORAK'S CORNER

February 17
Leicester City 1 Portsmouth 1
Scorer: Taylor (65)
Crowd: 31,775

Team: Hislop, Harper, Taylor, De Zeeuw, Primus, Foxe, Quashie, Sherwood, Merson, Todorov (Diabate), Aiyegbeni (Pericard). Substitutes: Kawaguchi, Festa, O'Neil.

A wonderful goal by Matthew Taylor in the 65th minute strike cancelled out Benjamin's early goal for Leicester to leave both teams ahead of the rest in the race for promotion. A draw was a fair result. Dickov could have scored another early in the second half, after a poor back pass from Tim Sherwood had left him with only goalkeeper Hislop to beat, but, ten minutes later, Merson's pass picked out Taylor wide on the left and he cut inside two defenders to crack home with his right foot.

February 22

MAKE GOALS, NOT WAR

It was hard not to feel a glow of pride. A well-organised squad, tidy at the back, eager to come forward. Yes, the Pompey For Peace movement (POFORP) made its presence felt in the great anti-war rally.

There they were – all members of the Pompey Anorak Brigade – dribbling down London's Shaftesbury Avenue last week carrying a banner made out of a blue bed sheet inscribed with 'Pompey for Peace' in yellow. It took five hours to get from Gower Street to Hyde Park and even wannabe Pompey fans, such as Tony Benn and the Rev Jesse Jackson, had gone home before they got there.

That's not all: there was a representative in Berlin and Berne, a rumour of one in Sydney, and the sighting of a blue-and-white bobble-hat outside the British Embassy in Prague. Such is their opposition to George Dubya Bush's attempts to disrupt the end of the season, a cadre of activists gathered on Monday to watch

MAN OF THE YEAR: Defender Linvoy Primus was Player of the Month four times and Player of the Year.

WANTED MAN: Harry Redknapp wanted to sign Tim Sherwood all season, and finally got his man in February .

WATER WAY TO GO: *Pompey lost their unbeaten home league record to Leicester in a lake! Above: Matthew Taylor. Below: Mark Burchill.*

BARGAIN BOY: Matthew Taylor was a steal at £750,000. His marauding runs down the left provided dynamic width.

WELL DONE, MATE: *Hayden Foxe, a Redknapp capture from West Ham and below, Nigel Quashie, who surrendered the captaincy to Merson.*

HOT STUFF, TODDY: Svetoslav Todorov celebrates yet another goal with the enthusiastic Matthew Taylor.

FEED THE YAK exhorted the fans, and they did. Aiyegbeni Yakubu scored 6 goals in eleven starts.

FOLK HERO: Super Paul Merson, the man who made the difference with his one-touch passing and brilliant vision.

the game against Leicester City in a pub within jeering distance of the American Embassy.

They rehearsed a new protest mantra: "No short corners. Not in our name" as yet another Paul Merson/Matt Taylor double act ricocheted off a defender. Stirring times then for the Pompey Anoraks, who owe their existence to 29-year-old Jamie Kennea. He was a Pompey exile in Birmingham, studying for his PhD, when he decided to contact fellow fans to share the thrills and, in those days, misery, of supporting Portsmouth.

From the University of California, where he now works as an astronomer, he said: "It was lonely going to away games by myself, without anyone to share the commiserations or celebrate with.

"I'm a bit tricky with computers so I set up a web link. That was six years ago this week, and about ten people joined. Now there are 565."

This season, of all seasons, he has not seen one game. On Saturdays, he gets up at dawn to listen on the internet and clicks on to his own website, which is buzzing with the key issues. Is Shaka Hislop commanding enough in the box? Is Kevin Harper better than Matthew Taylor? Are Hayden Foxe and Linvoy Primus good enough for the top flight? Should Paul Merson have a shave?

More importantly, the site has drawn together other lonely, dispossessed Pompey supporters – particularly those in exile from the south coast. No more are the train journeys to Fratton Park a long day's journey into the fright of losing 1-0 to Grimsby Town or struggling to draw with Stockport County. Now, every other Saturday is party time. Should you join the 11.08 from Waterloo on a match-day morning, you will find yourself in the company of some shrewd, high-powered mugs. Philosophers all.

The conversation is what you'd expect from Justin, a

haematologist from Hemel Hempstead, Nick, an expert in intellectual property, a smattering of headmasters, Andy, a careers officer, Simon, who creates video games, and a shipping broker based in the Dordogne who pops over occasionally.

Chat flows effortlessly from talking about Portsmouth to, er... talking about Portsmouth. But as Foster's are downed, there are diversions.

Weeks ago, while Londoners were agonising over the onset of new traffic regulations, Pompey Fans For Congestion Charges (POFORCON) were unanimous that Ken Livingstone was on to a good thing. There was an uncharacteristic flight into showbiz. Have there been any English actresses more sexy than Liz Taylor? Jean Simmons, Anna Neagle, Vivien Leigh (but only in *Spartacus*), and Bonnie Langford were rated, but not Catherine Deneuve, presumably on the grounds that she is Welsh. Glamour and Portsmouth don't really go together, so POFORGLAM is yet to be formed, but someone ventured, rather wistfully, that Amanda Holden might have come from Portsmouth, and there was talk of a group who called themselves Fratton Fred and the Frogmore Five, but I think that was a wind-up.

The other week, Nick, who is taking his five-month old daughter to today's game against Gillingham, went on a crazed riff about how great it would be if Pompey had a real slump, scraped into the play-offs, were down to 10 men in the final and won promotion on penalties. It was only when he realised that it meant going to Cardiff, the Baghdad of the West, that he realised what a bad idea it was.

What really passes the time is naming favourite players (or POFORPLAY – Pompey Fans for Players Past), although shaming the real disasters is much more fun, and, in Pompey's case, takes a lot longer. Everyone likes Paul Walsh, Nick went for Alan Biley – never to be forgotten for the two goals he scored in stoppage time against Oxford United after a pitch invasion by a Father Christmas. Nicky Jennings picked up a vote, and Dave went for Mike Trebilcock. Everyone rubbished Ian Baird and Warren Aspinall and all agreed that no team would be complete without the legendary Johnny Lager – or John Durnin, as his name appeared on the teamsheet.

I went for Albert McCann, who had been a midfield tyro in the Sixties, rather unkindly remembered for his bandy legs.

"Oh," said Pete. "McCann was a hit with my mum."

Must have been the bandy legs. (McCann's, not Pete's mum's.)

ANORAK'S CORNER

February 22
Portsmouth 1 Gillingham 0
Scorer: De Zeeuw (57)
Crowd: 19,428
Team: Hislop, Primus, De Zeeuw, Festa, Taylor, Quashie, Harper (O'Neil), Sherwood, Todorov, Aiyegbeni (Pericard), Merson. Substitutes: Kawaguchi, Diabate.

Dutch defender De Zeeuw scored his first goal of the season when he crashed in a header from the far post to head after a free kick from Merson. It was the biggest crowd of the season but not the best game. Gillingham, masterminded by player-manager Andy Hessenthaler, gave Portsmouth little opportunity to play, and there were few shots on goal.

CHAPTER 8

MARCH

March 1

WING AND A PRAYER

It was only to be expected. What sounded like a barrage of boos spread around the ground after the scrappy win against Gillingham. Puzzling to an outsider who could see that it wasn't exactly championship stuff but a win, nonetheless. But it wasn't a boo, it was a zoo. It was a tribute to Arjan De Zeeuw, the defender, whose every move is greeted with an appreciative "zooooo".

So you can imagine how it was when he scored the winning goal with a bone-crunching header. They've never gone much for booing at Fratton Park. Even in the dark days of relegation-threatened mediocrity the crowd would accept the team's shortcomings as long as they played bravely. That was why it was so shocking that Paul Merson was jeered for an indifferent patch and so unfair that Kevin Harper, the right wing back, has been the subject of abuse. Merson muttered about walking out; Harper just got on with it. Guess what? He has become a Fratton favourite – almost as popular as Matthew Taylor, his left flank counterpart. Taylor has been received with rapture right from the first kick of the season, and, after a couple of wonderful goals, fortunately captured on TV, against Nottingham Forest and Leicester City, the cry went up: "Taylor for England."

Taylor, 21, was indirectly responsible for football's quote of the season. Joe Kinnear, his erstwhile manager at Luton Town, described the price Harry Redknapp paid for him as highway robbery and bridled: "At least Dick Turpin had the decency to wear a mask." Kinnear, who brought Taylor through the youth team, tried everything he could to keep him.

"When I realised he had to go, I wanted a million for him," he said. "Pompey offered £150,000 but in the end they paid £600,000 in one go, £100,000 if he won an England cap, £100,000 if they got promoted, and another £150,000 depending [on] the number of games played. We get 20 per cent of any sell-on." Given that the official Portsmouth line was that they paid a starting price of £450,000, it looks like Joe picked the pocket of Highwayman Harry.

Kinnear said: "I thought he might become another Malcolm Macdonald, who started at left back with Luton and moved to centre forward. I could see Taylor as a striker because he loves coming forward and he's got the right brand of confidence and arrogance."

If Taylor turns out to be Redknapp's most successful long-term buy, Harper might be one of the best "left-overs" from last year. The 27-year-old Scot didn't make even the substitutes' bench at the start of the season, and was jeered because he tried to beat too many defenders and invariably failed to make the last pass.

When home fans boo an opposition player, the tendency is for him to play better, but as Mike Berry, senior lecturer in psychology at Manchester Metropolitan University, said: "Being jeered by your own side can drastically undermine you. A lot depends if the other players and manager are supportive and help him get over the feeling of isolation and lack of confidence." Harper has found support from a belief in God.

"I'm back to going to chapel every Sunday," he said. "I believe in God so much that without God it's impossible for me to do anything. I believe it's helping me to play better." No doubt Jim Smith, the assistant manager who knew Harper from their Derby days, has also helped. Harper's reward was a new two-year contract and a place in the Scotland B squad that drew with Turkey this week. Matthew Taylor's will no doubt be an under-21 cap, and, who knows, a full England place.

Mick Quinn, the former Portsmouth striker who commentates for 107.4 The Quay, the local radio station, said: "He reminds me of Kenny Sansom and he got 86 caps. I'd put Taylor ahead of Ashley Cole and Wayne Bridge. He could go to the top."

That would be something worth zooing about.

ANORAK'S CORNER

March 1
Millwall 0 Portsmouth 5
Scorers: Aiyegbeni (15, 25), Sherwood (31), Todorov (45), Merson (72 pen)
Crowd: 9,697
Team: Hislop, Primus, De Zeeuw, Festa, Taylor, Sherwood, Quashie, Harper (Crowe), Merson (Diabate), Todorov (Pericard), Aiyegbeni. Substitutes: Kawaguchi, O'Neil.

Lots of good football, but no fans to see it. The away supporters were banned because of violent scenes away from the ground last season and missed a devastating first half as Portsmouth raced to a 4-0 lead with two goals from Yakubu, Sherwood and a net-ripper from Todorov. Quashie and Millwall's Wise provided alternative entertainment with a punch up, which could easily have resulted in both being sent off. Millwall gave it a shot after the interval but once Hislop had made a couple of top saves, Yakubu was fouled and Merson scored a penalty. The Millwall fans gave Merson a standing ovation when he was substituted in the 81st minute and then they went home. You wondered why they stayed so long.

March 4
Wimbledon 2 Portsmouth 1
Scorer: Merson (26)
Crowd: 10,356
Team: Hislop, Primus, Crowe (O'Neil), De Zeeuw, Festa, Taylor, Quashie, Sherwood, Todorov (Pericard), Aiyegbeni, Merson.
Substitutes: Kawaguchi, Diabate.

More than 9,000 fans made the trip, no doubt hoping for a glimpse of the skills that destroyed Millwall the week before. It was not to be. Pompey scarcely had a shot on goal until the 26th minute when Merson scored from the edge of the box after a pass from Todorov. Wimbledon battled back in the second half; Agyemang equalised in the 65th minute and Ainsworth got the winner with four minutes to go. Suddenly, the massed voices of the Pompey choir were stilled.

March 8

THE CHEER READER

The perfect bookshop. What bliss. Long, dark aisles lined with Rudyard Kipling, darkly shrouded first editions of Dickens, yards of George Eliot, Biggles jostling with Harry Potter, Patricia Cornwell pitting her wits against Conan Doyle.

Like all good bookshops, there's a big outdoor porch with shelves of books – three for £1 and a sign inviting OAPs to help themselves. There are posters for organ recitals and – here's a clue – a flyer for tattooists. This is the shop where Portsmouth's biggest, loudest, most extrovert, most tuneless and most tattooed fan, John Portsmouth Football Club Westwood (he changed his name by deed poll), plies his trade.

His father started the business in 1959 and it is as tranquil a spot as Fratton Park is noisy. It is where John 'Jekyll' Westwood finishes his day, pours a cup of tea, and talks about his latest antiquarian book bargains. Over his head, a charter from the Prince of Wales confirms the shop as an official picture framer, by royal appointment. Alongside is his mother's collection of Victorian dolls.

But this mecca of philosophy and deep thought is abandoned when there's a game on. Every time Portsmouth play, John 'Hyde' Westwood takes over from the book-loving introvert – a demented bugle-playing, bell-ringing, chanting monster in blue wig, blue and white checked top hat, matching trousers and waistcoat. Fuelled with a pint or two from the nearby Newcome Arms, he becomes the club's unofficial cheer leader, exhorting players and fans alike to greater effort. "Gissa song," he implores the South Stand from his eyrie in the centre of the stand and even they – reticent souls – murmur a few polite chords of the *Pompey Chimes*.

They are noisier in the Fratton End: *"Portsmouth 'til I Die"* they sing, and John sings it louder and with more conviction than most because, quite simply, his life revolves around the club. Luckily his two children are following in father's footsteps – proud Pompey fans both.

He started supporting in 1976 when he was 12 (1-0 victory over Brighton in front of 32,000) and was hooked.

"There is a passion about the fans, which I don't find anywhere else. It could be something to do with the naval tradition and the fact that Portsmouth is actually an island. There's a sort of togethernesss about the place. This is a tight-knit community.

"I used to wear a rosette and carry a rattle, then I took to wearing all the gear like the top hat because I enjoy turning the game into a carnival." What elevates Westwood into Supporter Superstar is his bugle playing. It's terrible.

Richard Morrison, *The Times* music critic, trying vainly to help me describe the noise, suggested a likeness to the works of Stockhausen – like twiddling the dials of a short wave wireless backward and forward was his summation. I settled for an entire cattery being put down without anaesthetic.

Pompey coach Andy Awford offered to pay for bugle lessons but the crowd would be stunned into silence if Westwod actually played *You Dirty Northern Bastard* in tune.

Then there are the tattoos. Every inch of his fairly substantial body is a tattooed tribute to Portsmouth FC. He overcame his fear of needles to have his first one in 1989 – a discreet affair on his arm depicting the caricature of the Pompey sailor mascot – and now he is a mass of *Play Up Pompeys*.

Of course, you see little of his battle colours when he is at work, though when he lovingly caressed one of his favourite books, Gilbert White's *History of Selborne*, it was hard not to notice that his knuckles are decorated with the word POMPEY.

"I love working with books. My favourites are Camden's *Britannica,* which is an atlas book from 1605, Mudie's *History of Hampshire*, which came out in about 1850, and Isaak Walton's *Compleat Angler.*"

His mobile rings to the jubilant ring of the *Pompey Chimes.* "Yes, Mum, I won't be long," he promises, and we move from books to Biley.

"I liked Alan Biley, he was the cheeky chappie of the Eighties. Paul Walsh was like a god and I have so much respect for Alan Knight (who kept goal for 21 years from 1978). So many players lack loyalty these days."

He admires Milan Mandaric, the chairman who has spent millions since he bought the club in 1999. When he threatened to leave, John paid him a visit and begged him to stay.

"I know his wife doesn't want to leave," he confides. "I just want us to win everything and we need him to do that."

As Horace, the Roman poet whose works have graced the Petersfield Bookshop (but who would most certainly have not been a supporter of Pompey, the Roman general), almost commented in *Ars Poetica*: "Not gods, not men, not even booksellers, put up with players being second best."

ANORAK'S CORNER

March 12

Portsmouth 3 Norwich 2

Scorers: Aiyegbeni (57), Todorov (59, 72)

Crowd: 19,221

Team: Hislop, Primus, De Zeeuw, Festa, Taylor, Quashie (Diabate), Harper (O'Neil), Sherwood, Todorov, Aiyegbeni, Merson (Foxe). Substitutes: Kawaguchi, Pericard.

A dour, scrappy first half, a vibrant second half with Norwich unlucky to be beaten by an opportunist strike by Todorov. Norwich struck back within seconds each time Portsmouth went ahead with goals by Yakubu and Todorov. Todorov made it a lucky win with a vicious hooked shot from close quarters.

March 19

PRIMUS KEEPS THE FAITH

The Paulsgrove Estate in Portsmouth has had its share of hostile publicity. It was built after the war, when the city was devastated, and still has prefabs, tired council dwellings and an air of defiance, which comes, perhaps, from being slightly remote from the city. It has been the scene of angry demonstrations against paedophiles, it suffers from high unemployment, there are too many single mothers, and the curse of what the police call "anti-social" behaviour. There is a lot of crime, car theft and petty damage. It can be rough.

Once a fortnight, though, the playing fields ring to the sound of happy laughter and excited shouts of children playing football. It is part of a small experiment to deflect young people from a possible life of crime and help them to find a purpose in their sometimes difficult lives.

The organisers are members of the church and the referees are local policemen, but despite that possible inhibition to their idea of a good time, the children turn out in their scores because what really makes the evening come alive is a footballer with mighty dreads and a big smile. It's Portsmouth's cult hero, Linvoy Primus. And by Portsmouth, I mean the city just as much as the club because Primus has become as big a personality off the pitch as on. The supporters love him because he was under-rated, because he gives 101 per cent and because he is the one who turns up at public dos and is clearly seen to be trying to join in with the community.

Isn't it great when things don't go according to plan? At the beginning of the season, Harry Redknapp had his defence lined up: Eddie Howe from Bournemouth, Arjan De Zeeuw and Hayden Foxe had already signed, Gianluca Festa was about to. The best that Primus could hope for was a career on the bench, and even that appeared to be dashed in September when Redknapp drew him to one side to tell him that he had no future at the club. But nine minutes into the first game of the season, Howe limps off, Primus races on, and now only four players have turned out more often this season than he has.

He's a born-again footballer – you should have seen him charging down the right wing against Norwich City this week – and a born-again Christian whose faith is more important to him than his football.

He arrived in Portsmouth three years ago after humdrum years with Barnet and Reading, and didn't exactly shine until this season. Already he has been the supporters' player of the month three times, despite playing much of the season with a groin injury, and this month was voted best defender in the Nationwide League. Recently, Harry drew him to one side and offered him a new contract.

He said: "I found the self-pride to do well after Mick Mellows (a Portsmouth player from the Seventies) invited me to a church meeting, and I have learnt the importance of serving the Lord with all my heart," he said. "I found, by playing for God, it lifted the hassle, the burden, of trying to impress my bosses here.

"When I have played well, I have felt that there has been something extra added, pushing me to a level which is now the best of my career. Mick got me helping with the kids on the estate, which is a possible trouble spot and has a few problems. Playing football and having a knockabout gives the kids a bit of hope, and it helps them learn that the police are not the enemy. It involves parents and the community. I don't do very much apart from sign autographs and do a little coaching."

Sergeant Fiona Voller of the local police station has nothing but praise for Primus. "Linvoy has been like a superstar," she said. "His contribution is fantastic. He joins in, giggling with the kids, signs autographs and does a little teaching. He is such a wonderful example and the children think it's great that such a famous footballer actually comes to see them. I'm sure it's because of his influence that the referees never get booed and it helps to stop the children thinking about the police as being 'the pigs'."

Primus, 29, who is married with three children, discovered his faith about 18 months ago and is certain he would not be doing this kind of work if he had been asked, say, two years ago. I might have done it for the recognition but now I realise how important it is that these kids have something different in their lives," he said.

"I don't know what God has lined up for me when I give up but it won't be in football but in the real world, perhaps working with deprived kids. Now, I have the joy of playing football as well as the happiness of having God in my life.

"In the long run, my faith is what matters. I have to say, God is more important to me than Mr Redknapp."

I'm sure Harry will forgive him.

ANORAK'S CORNER

March 15
Portsmouth 1 Wolverhampton Wanderers 0
Scorer: Stone (4)
Crowd: 19,558
Team: Hislop, Primus (Harper), De Zeeuw, Festa, Foxe, Sherwood, O'Neil, Stone, Todorov (Burton), Aiyegbeni (Diabate), Merson. Substitutes: Kawaguchi, Pericard.

The best crowd of the season, though not the best game. Stone celebrated his recall to the side for the first time in two months with the only goal in the fourth minute then he ran most of the opposition half, skipped through the defence and beat the goalkeeper. And that was that. Neither goalkeeper had to make a serious save all game and the Portsmouth defence, particularly Foxe, were well in control.

March 19
Coventry 0 Portsmouth 4
Scorers: og (14), Stone (17), Harper (23), Merson (68)
Crowd: 13,922
Team: Hislop, Foxe, De Zeeuw (Heikkinen), Festa, Stone (Diabate), Harper, Sherwood, O'Neil, Todorov (Pericard), Aiyegbeni, Merson.
Substitutes: Kawaguchi, Burton.

It was all over after 23 minutes as Portsmouth extended their lead at the top of the league to five points. The Coventry defence were terrible and the Portsmouth defence stayed sound. Merson rounded things off in the second half, gratefully receiving a back heel from Todorov and scoring with a rare left footer. Merson, whose 35th birthday was the following day, speculated that to get 100 points and score 100 goals this season was a distinct possibility. Redknapp thought winning more points than anyone else would do nicely.

March 22
WHISPERING THE C-WORD

It is time to come out of the closet. The P word has lost its shock value. Promotion? Piece of cake. Now for the C word. I wouldn't use it if it was at all gratuitous, so here goes: champions.

It's not a word used often by Portsmouth fans, whose team were last champions in 1962 and 1983, in the old Third Division. No need for a cabinet for all that silverware, a cupboard under the Chimes Bar would do. Now, the fans are sloughing off years of collective depression and using the C word with reckless abandon.

It trembled on the lips in 1987 when Pompey were in contention for much of the season before being pipped to top spot in the First Division by Derby County – well, pipped by six points. The team was a rough, tough, combative side moulded, cajoled and kept together by Alan Ball. It was an unfashionable side at a time when football was unpopular, with attendances rarely creeping much above the 10,000 mark.

But Portsmouth fans rather like unfashionable (or they did until this season) and there is a generation that swoons with nostalgia at the mention of Kenny Swain, Kevin Dillon, Paul Hardyman, Mick Tait (who, over seven years, played in every shirt bar goalkeeper), Noel Blake and Micky Quinn. Who will ever forget the mercurial wing work of Vince Hilaire or Mick Kennedy, the man who summed up the sheer non-stop energy of the team? Always in trouble, always scrapping, always playing to win.

Kennedy, a football coach for youngsters in County Clare, Ireland, said: "I still get a thrill thinking about that season. I remember every game, every minute, every second. It was a great achievement and Alan Ball kept us all together. People said we were difficult, but we weren't really." Kennedy maintains that the team were nothing like as bad as they were made out to be, and confided to a supporters' club meeting: "If we kicked someone, it was meant nicely."

Hilaire, who coaches and commentates on The Quay, the local radio station, said: "Fratton Park was a frightening place then – Fortress Fratton we called it – and my team relied more on intimidation than they do today. We were much more physical than today's side, though I think they would beat us on technique and ability.

"I wouldn't get in this team, because of the extra demands on the players. I'm not sure I would be getting back in defence like Matthew Taylor and still be able to operate on the wing the way I used to."

Hilaire happily admits that the team of 1987 were well-known in the game for partying and having a good time – but within limits. "There was no drinking before the game, or even on Thursday, though I have to admit, when we were allowed out, we took it to the extreme. Bally knew how to handle us and he encouraged us to compete to get our attitude right. There were more fights on the training ground between the players than at any other time.

"It's completely different now. Players are professional, conscientious and well behaved. On the other hand, they get more money and some of them don't mind being left out of the team because they aren't as hungry as we were. I played my first game in 1977 and the best way for a manager to assert his discipline was to drop you from the first team. That really hurt your pride – and you lost your match bonus."

After the C word, the S word. Survival. Are Portsmouth good enough to stay in the Premiership? "Everyone talks about Harry Redknapp and his wheeler dealing, but they overlook the technical nous he and Jim Smith bring to the game," Hilaire said. "These two are the wiliest brains in football and will already know who they want for next season to stay in the Premiership."

Anyway, that's next season. Now we are heading for party time. Hilaire and Kennedy regret losing the last game of the season and not going up on a high. "To be honest, we had been up late the night before," Kennedy said. "After the game we partied all night – and then all week."

ANORAK'S CORNER

March 22
Preston 1 Portsmouth 1
Scorer: Aiyegbeni (5)
Crowd: 16,665
Team: Hislop, Foxe, Primus, Festa, Stone, Harper, O'Neil, Sherwood, Todorov, Aiyegbeni, Merson.
Substitutes: Kawaguchi, Heikkinen, Diabate, Clarke.

When Primus, of all people, almost scored with a stinging volley after three minutes and Yakubu did actually hit the net after five, it seemed Pompey would win at Deepdale for the first time in 31 years. Irritatingly, Preston gave as good as they got and McKenna equalised with two minutes to go. This was the anniversary of Redknapp's first game in charge (a 2-0 defeat by Preston) and he was on good form: "It was my first game, I didn't have much of a team and didn't fancy the job too much, but I was skint. But a year on, it's gone great."

March 29

DOING THE BUSINESS

It was different then. Fathers would hide their sons' eyes as they trudged past the The Pompey Hotel just outside the quaint main gates of Fratton Park. It was bulging with beery supporters, spilling out on to the pavement clutching pints of Mr Brickwood's finest.

These days, youngsters are dragging their parents in to spend their cash, not on pints, but on shirts, mugs, pens, scarves, ashtrays, beanie babies and tracksuit bottoms. It's the Pompey Shop and it is making a fortune. This week, Tara Snowden, who runs the place, was able to tell her boss that the profit has rocketed from £800,000 last year to £2 million this. OK, it's not exactly the financial bedrock to guarantee survival in the Premiership next season, but the sale of 41,000 team strips – yours for £39.99 – gives a glimpse into the commercial revolution that has hit the old place.

Tara's boss is Peter Storrie, a long-time mate of Harry Redknapp from West Ham days, when they were chief executive and manager respectively.

When Storrie took the job at Portsmouth two years ago, he seemed just the latest of a quick turnover of chief executives who came and went as fast as chairman Milan Mandaric hired and fired his managers. The club's wage bill was rising – in 2001 it was 64 per cent up on the previous year – and the pre-tax loss over the two years was about £10 million.

Storrie, whose office is an undistinguished box with a glimpse of a corner of the ground, a picture of HMS Victory hanging slightly askew on the wall, his lunchtime sandwiches in the fridge, said: "I had a sneaking feeling we might be able to do something.

"Harry persuaded me to come here, but when I first walked

in the door, it was like stepping back in time, like it had been with West Ham in 1989, with an old stadium and old ways of working. There's a saying in football: 'People have always done it that way', and that was the attitude here." He found a staff that had been "pushed under" and not allowed to manage.

One of his predecessors was so hands-on that he insisted on overseeing every detail, even down to cancelling an order for new envelopes because they had a stock of A4 ones.

The evidence of his regime was immediate. Fans arriving for the first home game of the season were struck by the proliferation of new advertising hoardings and a touch of smartness thanks to a few licks of paint here and there.

"I found there were people with a lot of good ideas, and many of them have since blossomed, but there were a lot from the 'freebie club'. Whatever it was they were doing, it was for themselves, not for the football club. They just liked the idea of the tickets and the prestige."

This season, with capacity crowds and more TV money than before, the club has just about matched its hugely inflated wage bill. But what about next season? Will promotion be the worst thing that could happen to the club? Can it avoid the financial catastrophes that have befallen Ipswich Town, Bradford City and Coventry City?

"This is the best possible time to go up," he said. "Wages and transfers are spiraling down and I have negotiated contracts with a differential written into them so that the players get more for playing in the Premiership and less in the First Division.

"The secret is to be sensible, to set budgets and abide by them. If we can't afford Fred, we won't have him. I think of the Premier as three mini divisions. There is Manchester United and that lot at the top, a middle batch and then there's the bottom eight and that's the 'division' we have to win. I have to think we are better than the two we are going up with and that we can beat some of the bottom teams. There is no point thinking we are going to go straight to the top. If we can finish sixteenth, that's an achievement. Then we might edge up a position or two and maybe in a few years' time, we could reach the top ten.

"The example set by Charlton is definitely the way forward and I think the vast majority of Pompey supporters would go for that. They don't want another administration and a debt of £16 million.

"Just think, finishing fourth from bottom is worth £17 million. We are going to spend. We need about five or six players to strengthen the squad and because of what is going on in the game at the moment there will be a lot of players available here and in Europe."

The supporters will be pleased to hear that he and Harry want to take up the option to buy young Nigerian striker Yakubu Aiyegbeni for a reported £4 million.

"Harry and I are quite a team, we don't lose many once we have decided to get them. Harry chooses them, I do the deal. Harry isn't given the credit for picking the players in the first place. Look at Matthew Taylor, who he found playing for Luton; he will probably be playing for England within 12 months. He doesn't mind taking a gamble. Hiring Merson was a fantastic gamble, so was Foxey [Hayden Foxe]. But they have been monsters for us.

"Harry's football mad."

The big gap in Storrie's plans is the lack of a Premiership-size stadium. By nicking space here and there and squeezing in seats wherever he can, the capacity will reach 20,000 next season, still one of the smallest in the First Division, let alone the Premiership.

Success on the pitch has stifled criticism of the way the club has yet to announce definite plans for a new ground. It has become a long running joke (for about four years) that the official statement will be made "next week".

"We'll have a stadium," Storrie said. "I can't do anything more commercially until it is built. We have only 250 executive seats, with people paying between £2,000 and £4,500 per season. Imagine how much we would make if we had 1,000 seats."

After years as a West Ham supporter – he was born 500 yards from Upton Park – he has been won over by the supporters and has embarked on a 'love affair' with Portsmouth Football Club.

"If we meet West Ham next year, it's Pompey for me, not West Ham."

Everything is geared to next season. Back in the shop, Tara Snowden plans a limited-edition promotion strip and a new range of blue and white babywear. As the saying goes: "Give me a child for the first seven years and you have a Pompey fan (and his money) for life".

More from 'Arry's Bargain Basement. No sooner had Ipswich announced that their whole team was up for sale – they are £60 million in the red and in administration – than he was in for their doughty defender Hermann Hreidarsson for a reported £750,000. That's big money, in fact, it would be his biggest buy yet.

By the way, Harry's very des. res. overlooking the harbour at Poole, Dorset, is on the market. It has a grand marble hallway with a double staircase, balconies overlooking the bay, chandeliers and lots of black, cream and gold. It's yours for £3.25 million – about twice what he spent creating his team.

CHAPTER 9

APRIL

April 5

THE MELLOWING OF MERSON

A sunny spring morning and a father and his three boys are having a kickaround in a sports' club playing field. Dad lobs in obliging centres, which the boys hammer goalwards with an agility and control beyond their years. It must be something in the genes.

Well, dad is Paul Merson, whose flair and refusal to do the obvious has been the crucial difference between Portsmouth and the chasing pack, this season. They amble back to the pavilion, past waiting camera crews and a trio of autograph hunters, to get stuck into the mountains of pasta, which have been laid on for Merson's other lads – the Portsmouth team of which he is captain. This is Paul Merson, relaxed family man, team leader, father figure and strolling genius. If all had gone according to the plan of Graham Taylor, manager of Aston Villa, Merson would have spent the season on the subs bench, playing cameo roles.

After an Inter-Toto game in the summer, in which Merson

appeared as a sub, Taylor said: "That's the role I see you in." Merson said: "I don't see it." Taylor said: "That's the way it is." Within days, Merson was a Portsmouth player.

He said: "I wasn't sure it was a great move, but it was a challenge and I like a challenge; to see how I can do and push myself to the limit. Above all, I wanted to play and Harry Redknapp told me he was going to give it a right go. Mind you, when I saw the state of the training facilities," he gestures at the ill-prepared playing fields, where he and his boys had been having their kickabout after the club's training session, "I thought: 'Oh, my God'.

"And, when we were 2-0 down at Crystal Palace at the start of the season, I walked off at half time wondering, 'what the hell am I doing here?'"

What he has been doing there is to help Portsmouth have their most exciting season for more than 50 years. With the clarity of hindsight, 39 wins, 82 goals and 83 points later, I can safely say that I thought promotion beckoned about 15 minutes into the first game of the season when he flicked a trademark one-touch pass into the path of Deon Burton. Okay, Burton was offside, but it was a moment of poetry, a rare commodity at Fratton Park.

Last month, he celebrated his 35th birthday and faced up to the intimations of footballing mortality. He is clearly tempted to reprise this role of fading but fabulous Svengali. It's a trick that has been done before.

Brian Clough brought in the great Dave MacKay from Tottenham, and Derby stormed to promotion. Stuart Pearce did something like it for Manchester City. Paul Ince was brought in this season to do what Merse has done for Portsmouth.

He said: "I would do like to this again." He adds, rather shyly, given the enormity of the boast: "If I was with Wolves this season, they would have got promoted. They would have gone up. I would also like to have a go as a player-manager too, that would be nice."

The rejection by Villa clearly rankles. "I do want to play in the Premiership. I have something to prove and I would like to try my wits. But, yeah, in the long run I would like to be a manager." When he joined, did he see the season taking off like this?

"Naah. I thought maybe we'd get in the play-offs. When you put a whole new team together, you think it might take 10 games to settle in and hope to put a run together. You can buy all the players in the world, but if you ain't got the manager or the coach, it doesn't work. The manager takes the credit. He didn't just buy a whole load of players and think 'now let's make a team out of this'. He picked his team – bang, bang, bang – for each position, and he did it perfectly. Then he put me in as the last bit of the jigsaw behind the front two. When I played my first training games, the lads said 'wow' because they could see how it was going to work.

"You can imagine him sitting in the stands last season when he was director of football working out who he wanted. Getting Toddy (Svetoslav Todorov from West Ham) was brilliant, he's too good for this division.

"Harry is the best. He wanted to buy me at Middlesbrough when I was having a bad time but he couldn't afford me. We have played entertaining football and every player is playing well above their station – if they hadn't, they wouldn't be here now. I know it sounds horrible, but that's football."

Now, with his short hair and tidy beard, he's getting used to the idea of being the older statesman. "I have a responsibility to the others. When you get to 35, you have to set an example by talking to them on the pitch and teaching during training. They listen and they are enthusiastic. I like to help the lads such as Gary O'Neil and Nigel Quashie. They can go on to better

things, maybe even play for England

Yes, that's Paul Merson talking, football's Mr Respectable, sipping litres of orange juice, surrounded by his boys. Merson had one sticky patch in the season when he played on with a damaged ankle and underperformed. So much so, a section of the crowd booed him. "I shouldn't have played but I wanted to because it's hard to know when to rest, especially as I am coming to the point when I won't be playing much longer.

"I was disappointed at the time – how could they do this to me? – but when you think they have had years of crowds of only 15,000 for five years and now have 20,000, I'm sure the ones who were booing were the newcomers."

He understands the innate pessimism of the Pompey fans, who sees a dark lining in every silver cloud, because he admits to being a bit of a pessimist himself.

"Everyone is greedy for success. They say they will be OK with 40 points next season, but if it's the same the season after, it becomes dangerous, and then the chairmen start whacking out money right, left and centre, bringing in £5-million players. Then you get 39 points and you're relegated.

"But, yeah, this has been fun, but then it's our job to be fun." And to bring a little poetry into our lives. The supporters are voting for the player of the season. The poets among them will have to go for Merse. One of them actually wrote a poem in *True Blue*, the fanzine, dedicated to 'our skipper and inspiration.' That's Merse, from worse to verse.

ANORAK'S CORNER

April 5

Walsall 1 Portsmouth 2

Scorers: Harper (15), Todorov (33)

Crowd: 7,899

Team: Hislop, Primus, Festa, Foxe, Sherwood, Quashie, Stone, Harper, Todorov, Aiyegbeni (Burton), Merson.

Substitutes: Kawaguchi, O'Neil, Heikkinen, Diabate.

An unconvincing win, enlivened by a wonderful solo goal by Harper and the sight of Sherwood jinking past two defenders and centring to Todorov to score his 19th of the season with an easy header. Probably the most significant event of the day was Yakubu limping off with a torn hamstring to be replaced by the anonymous Burton. Walsall scored on half time and the second half was a scrappy affair with Merson stumbling when he might have scored.

April 12

THE NAME'S BOND...

Relegation. Now there's a word. A familiar one to Portsmouth fans. Usually, at this stage of the season, they would be gloomily debating the odds on avoiding the drop over pints in the Artillery Arms and rehearsing rousing choruses of *The Great Escape* in the Newcome Arms.

Come the last game of the season, Portsmouth supporters are usually so exhausted by weeks of ulcer-inducing tension as the team scrape a draw here, manage a freak win there, that darkened rooms beckon and men in white suits are put on standby. It is a little different this year, but someone who has kept his head when faced with the two impostors of triumph and disaster is Kevin Bond. He is the one hovering off centre stage in the dugout behind Harry Redknapp and Jim Smith, and, as reserve-team coach, makes up the triumphant managerial triumvirate.

Bond, 46, was named assistant manager in 1998 after one of Portsmouth's greatest seasons; they finished twentieth with 49 points. Alan Ball took over as manager in January with the club reeling from the depredations of the Terry Venables era and seven points clear – at the bottom of the table.

His sheer blood-and-guts passion drove the team to safety.

Bond joined in the summer and found himself in yet another relegation battle – they finished with 47 points and the club in administration. Enter Milan Mandaric, the new chairman eager for the instant success that Ball and Bond had no chance of delivering. They were out by December. Bond has that phlegmatic approach to the vagaries of football life that so many in the game share. "It was all quite amicable," he said. "Milan thought things were moving too slowly and wanted to change. You can't bear grudges in football; it's a fact of life for all of us that we will, at some time, lose our job. We just have to be philosophical."

Bond went to West Ham United and became the overseas scout for his old boss, Harry Redknapp, for whom he had played at Bournemouth. "I have known him since I was 10 and our families [his father is John Bond, one-time West Ham stalwart, who played with Redknapp] know each other extremely well," Bond said. "When things went awry for the previous manager [Graham Rix], Harry asked me back for the second time around.

"I didn't think it would be as good as this or success as quick because although it is easy to buy, it's a lot more difficult to buy the right players and get the balance right. Harry is very astute in the transfer market, he has a very good eye. It is hard for a manager to find the time to check on players and he often has to rely on other people to find them.

Sometimes they turn out not to be quite what the manager had in mind. It's a mistake Harry does not make."

He may have the lowest profile of the trio, but to judge from the heated discussions he has with Redknapp and Smith during training sessions, his voice is heard and the players respect his training methods, enthusiasm for new exercise regimes and approach to the game.

"This is the kind of side I like to be associated with. I enjoy the passing game, the way we work through Paul Merson, and not just lumping the ball anywhere." A bit different from the old days of despair, then?

"No, Bally was the same, he liked footballing sides and people with spirit, and he was fabulous when he had his back to the wall, getting the team out of trouble. When you think of what he achieved with the financial mess he was in, it was a fantastic achievement."

Which players have surprised him? "I can't pick out any one. There's Matthew Taylor, who came out of nowhere to play for England Under-21s, Kevin Harper, who was treading water, Linvoy Primus has swum the Channel, Hayden Foxe was nowhere and now look at him.

"I would be hard pushed to say that we could have got more out of anybody, from the management team to the players. They've never left anything in the dressing-room."

There has been chatter on the Pompey Anorak's site that the *Pompey Chimes* have been drowned out by the effervescent "We are Toppa the League" and the ever popular "Harry 'n' Jim". The terrace tunesmiths should add to the repertoire with "Harry 'n' Jim 'n' Kevin."

By the way, if Portsmouth win today against Sheffield Wednesday, they are promoted. Promotion. That's a word I never thought I would write.

More from 'Arry's Bargain Basement. After a quiet spell he ran his eye over Wimbledon's Jobi McAnuff, Nigel Reo-Coker, Lionel Morgan and Damien Francis during their win

against Sheffield United, and he's bringing Roma defender
Saliou Lassissi over for a trial.

ANORAK'S CORNER

April 12

Portsmouth 1 Sheffield Wednesday 2
Scorer: Bradbury (18)
Crowd: 19,524
Team: Hislop, Festa, Foxe, Primus, Harper (De Zeeuw), Quashie,
Stone, Sherwood, Todorov, Bradbury, Merson.
Substitutes: Kawaguchi, O'Neil, Burton, Diabate.

*It was meant to be promotion party night. It ended in defeat
with a farcical extra-time goal, when Sheffield substitute Reddy not
only seized on Festa's mis-hit free kick to score, but knocked
Portsmouth off the top for the first time since August. Lee Bradbury,
in the team for the first time of the season, latched on to the ball
after the goalkeeper only parried Todorov's shot. Portsmouth had
two good chances from Bradbury, and Quashie saved in the second
half but lost the initiative when Westwood equalised with 14 minutes
to go.*

*Harry Redknapp was outraged at the winner: "I can take losing,
but not that. It was the most scandalous goal I've ever seen in
football. It was a farce. I spoke to the referee afterwards, but I don't
think he understood what he'd done. But I understood what he'd
done – he'd got it wrong."*

April 15
Portsmouth 1 Burnley 0
Scorer: Todorov (73)
Crowd: 19,221
Team: Hislop, Foxe, Primus, De Zeeuw, Festa, Quashie, Stone, Sherwood, Todorov, Bradbury (Pericard), Merson.
Substitutes: Kawaguchi, O'Neil, Diabate, Harper.

Portsmouth were promoted, thanks to a goal from Todorov in the 73rd minute. Quashie laid it on with a nicely paced low pass and Todorov hit it with his right foot to score his 20th goal of the season. It was a nervy evening. Merson missed a penalty and Bradbury fluffed two chances, but, at the end, an ecstatic crowd streamed on to the pitch to salute manager Redknapp before letting him and the team go on a riotous lap of honour.

Later the manager said: "Portsmouth will be my last club. I don't want to be doing it when I'm 70, like Sir Bobby Robson. I've had 20-odd years doing it, but I'll be here next season. I'm not going anywhere."

April 18
Ipswich Town 3 Portsmouth 0
Crowd: 29,396
Team: Hislop, Foxe, Primus, De Zeeuw (O'Neil), Festa, Quashie, Stone, Sherwood, Todorov, Bradbury (Pericard), Merson (Harper).
Substitutes: Kawaguchi, Diabate.

What an anti-climax. Instead of taking a decisive step to the First Division championship, a jaded Portsmouth were routed by Ipswich Town, who had to win to maintain their chances of reaching the play-offs. Pompey were three down within 30 minutes. It could have been more. Their supporters sang with fanatical zeal throughout, and Harry Redknapp said: "I never thought we would finish above Ipswich this season, but look at us. We're not Real Madrid, but we have still managed to get 89 points. We couldn't even train the other day because the training ground, which belongs to Southampton University, was locked."

April 19
AND NOW YOU WILL BELIEVE US

Phew. Some week. I have had so many people congratulating me. I thought I must have re-married in my sleep or been promoted at work. But no, it was much more important than that, it was Portsmouth that had been promoted and such is our relationship with football that even the humblest of fan becomes part of the action and identified with the success.

Ever since P-Day the papers have been at pains to point out how poorly Pompey will fare next season; ageing midfield trio of Merson, Stone and Sherwood, Primus not up to it, Shaka shaky, blah, blah, blah.

The commentator on BBC Five Live got it right though, with an almost rhapsodic riff about the fans, how they never stop ringing out the *Pompey Chimes*, how they brave fog-shrouded nights in Grimsby and cheer through rain-lashed afternoons in Port Vale. So, Premiership, watch out. If you had seen John PFC Westwood leading the 15-minute non-stop chant of 'Toppa the League, Harry 'n' Jim' like a crazed incantation to the gods, you would know that the players might not frighten you but you will tremble when you come face to face with the fans.

What is it about football clubs and their supporters? Every week, I phone up Paddy Thomas for my post-match debrief and conversation about the Saturday before. He has resigned as chairman of the supporters' club for the second time because of ill health. He is quietly spoken, a former head of science at a local grammar, and rational, yet he has given his time and love to the club, supporting it through years of failure, odd flashes of success, boardroom skullduggery and managerial chaos.

He is quietly libellous (and absolutely correct) about some of the dramatis personae who have strutted and slunk their way into Portsmouth history.

He has been a supporter since just before his ninth birthday in 1951.

"I didn't see much of my dad when I was little because he was posted to Japan with the RAF after the war but he took me to my first game. All I remember is the crowd and the atmosphere. My second game was memorable because I was late and passed down over the heads of the crowd. I was right at the front when Duggie Reid, one of the Pompey legends, who was on the halfway line, took two paces and hit the ball so hard he scored.

"When he was in a nursing home towards the end of his life, the supporters presented him with a wheelchair and I knelt by his side and said: 'you were my boyhood hero.'

"He couldn't talk but he squeezed my hand and gave me a smile.

"We used to play football in the morning and race to get to the ground when it opened at one, pulling our trousers over our shorts and muddy knees. There were two entrances marked boys – not children – then we'd wait two hours for the game to start. Even now I get to the ground early because I like the way the atmosphere gradually builds up."

After a spell in the Midlands, at college and teaching physics, he married and returned south. This was a moment of truth for his patient wife, Marlene, who comes from Wakefield, rugby league country.

"She saw what it meant to me and realised she would have to follow Pompey or find a new boyfriend."

He became chairman of the supporters' club and stayed in that role through some of the most cataclysmic times in the club's recent history, involving thwarted plans to build a new stadium, an unsuccessful take-over attempt and the club going into administration.

He had a fascinating insight into a brief, miserable, spell in the mid-Nineties, as notable for its creative accounting methods as its football.

"There was one transfer, which was valued at £250,000 though the club that bought the player claimed it had spent only £125,000. I was amazed to see that two of the Pompey negotiators had been paid £62,500 each, one of them for spending the weekend abroad assessing the player, and the other for 'obtaining the signature.'

"I resigned.

"Things have changed. There was a time when the fans were treated as though they were an irritant and the management were very confrontational.

"Milan Mandaric recognised the importance of fan power from the beginning and Peter Storrie, the chief executive, treats us with respect.

"Emotionally it has been the best-ever season. But I don't think anything will compare to those championship years. Jimmy Scoular, Jim Dickinson, Peter Harris – they were heroes to me."

Yakubu Aiyegbeni, Matthew Taylor, Nigel Quashie. Will they be remembered in 50 years' time? No doubt they are already heroes to countless nine-year-olds, for whom this season will also be beyond compare.

ANORAK'S CORNER

April 21
Portsmouth 3 Reading 0
Scorers: Pericard (19, 45), Todorov (71)
Crowd: 19,535
Team: Hislop, Foxe, Primus, Festa, Quashie (O'Neil), Stone, Harper (De Zeeuw), Sherwood, Todorov, Pericard, Merson (Diabate).

Substitutes: Kawaguchi, Burton.

Portsmouth went into the game knowing that Leicester had been defeated by Sheffield United and that a win would put them back on top of the league after a four-day absence. Pericard made sure they did with two fine first-half goals. The first came after a nippy run by Harper from midfield, the second when he struck on the rebound from his first shot. Todorov scored his 21st of the season when he ran from inside his own half at an indecisive defence before finding the corner of the net.

April 26
A VIEW FROM THE GENTS

It was rather sweet of the Ipswich Town DJ to play *Congratulations* for the visiting fans as they noisily celebrated promotion. Then he rather spoilt it by playing something, presumably more heartfelt, that had the chorus: *"We Don't Like You."*

The Pompey fans were so mellow that they hardly noticed Ipswich romping home 3-0, contenting themselves with the occasional chant of *"You're just a small town in Norwich,"* and a bravura performance by John PFC Westwood, cheerleader extra-ordinaire, who danced on a terrace roof leading a chant of *"Toppa the League, Harry 'n' Jim"* for 20 unrelenting minutes. Exhausted by the singing, we retired to the Drum and Monkey – a nearby hostelry recommended by the police. We were only half a pint in when a posse of Ipswich's finest hoved into view. A few jeers later and the pub was rocked by an almighty thud as a brick hit the window. Then another, and, next thing, showers of glass ricocheted across the bar, trembling children were lifted over the bar for safety, and our brave lads grabbed every chair they could to defend themselves as the Ipswich massive, who looked like extras from *Walking with Cavemen*, smashed their way in. I made a dash for the gents and cowered for safety behind a substantial woman, who could have been Jo Brand's bigger sister.

Minutes later, feeling rather ashamed at my cowardice, I crept back to the bar to be confronted by an astonishing sight of crumpled tables, shattered chairs, beer and glass everywhere, the jukebox overturned, some blood, weeping kids, furious fathers, and an Ipswich fan out cold on the floor.

What was that about, we wondered, as the police escorted us to the station? After all, their team had won. All very depressing, which is not a word you would apply to the City of Portsmouth. Talk about the feel-good factor, it's more the feel-fantastic factor. The city has been transformed.

"The place used to be so depressed, but now everything is different," Mike Hancock, MP for Portsmouth South, said. "It's good for the local economy if only because of the number of shirts and Pompey memorabilia being bought. Kids want a Portsmouth shirt with Merson on, rather than an England shirt with Beckham. Now we need a proper stadium – Portsmouth deserves that.

"It hasn't eased the situation for people with real problems who come to my surgeries, but it has given a lot of people great cheer."

There is endless cheer at the Newcome Arms – a favourite with supporters – where Nigel Tresidder, the landlord, has sold enough lager to float the Ark Royal.

He said: "The atmosphere is absolutely electric, the city is bubbling, it has gone mad," adding happily: "There has been a big increase in my takings – it has been phenomenal."

Even the business community is buoyed up. Maureen Newton, of the Chamber of Commerce, said: "We are hoping for more visitors to our pubs and restaurants. The name Portsmouth already has a higher profile as the city gets talked about more."

The city council is planning to research the impact that life in the Barclaycard Premiership will have and reckons that business confidence in Portsmouth is set to boom. Barbara Thompson, Director of Economic Regeneration and Tourism, said: "A really big spin-off for us is the huge media profile that Portsmouth will have now that matches are screened around the world. The BBC said that the Arsenal-Manchester United game would have been watched by one-sixth of the world's population. "The city now has a positive image and that may help us attract more business and new companies to the city."

The police are joining in too. A spokesperson confirmed the outbreak of feel-good factor, although it was not enough to reduce the normal level of crime. But she added: "In the last 12 months, we have seen a dramatic decrease in the level of burglaries – could there be a connection?"

Maybe Anthony Minghella, the film director and Pompey fan, whom I first met when the club was fighting bankruptcy and relegation, best summed up why promotion matters so much. He said: "The club is like a tree. Its roots spread into the life of the city. It affects transport, the pubs and clubs, the sales of newspapers, the trade in the shops. It is a focus for the community with an economic and cultural remit. When the team does well, there is a sense of wellbeing and of renewed identity."

Or, as the female taxi driver who dropped me at the station put it: "Everyone's happy. You should see my dad, he won't take his scarf off – he's over the moon."

ANORAK'S CORNER

April 27

Portsmouth 3 Rotherham United 2

Scorers: Merson (11 pen), Todorov (22, 45)

Crowd: 19,420

Team: Hislop, Foxe, Primus, Festa, Quashie, Stone, Harper (De Zeeuw), Sherwood, Todorov, Pericard (Aiyegbeni), Merson. Substitutes: Kawaguchi, O'Neil, Diabate.

This was it. Merson scored a penalty in the eleventh minute after Todorov was upended, and, after a helter-skelter first half that saw five goals, Pompey finished champions. They were buoyed by the news that Leicester had only managed a 1-1 draw with Norwich. Rotherham made it hard. They came back twice to make it 2-2. But two goals from Todorov saw Pompey take lead right on half time – and so it stayed. A crowd invasion, the presentation of the first piece of silverware for 20 years, the second lap of honour within a week, and Pompey were champions.

Milan Mandaric, who had been teasing the supporters with hints that he might leave the club and return to America, said: "I can't walk away now."

CHAPTER 10

MAY

May 3

WHERE IT ALL WENT WRONG

Here's a confession. This column should have been about Port Vale. Or Grimsby. Maybe Swansea. This is meant to be a discrete ghetto about a really unglamorous club, preferably bobbing about in the relegation zone, ideally in administration, the manager just given the chairman's vote of confidence. It is meant to be the antidote to all that unending stuff about the fat cats in the Premiership that so obsess sports editors.

So, it has gone badly wrong. What really wrecked the assignment is not just that Portsmouth are Nationwide Division One champions, but they won by playing attacking, passing football with gonnabe stars such as Matthew Taylor, Yakubu Aiyegbeni and Vincent Pericard (you wait), whose cosmopolitan glamour will be much talked-about next season.

There was nothing glamorous about my first game, which was, amazingly, 40-odd years ago. With a certain neatness, it was against Rotherham, stoic victims of Pompey's championship celebrations on Sunday.

They won that Sixties encounter too, though I have no doubt it was a terrible game with a Portsmouth team that included the great Jimmy Dickinson, Ron Saunders and Harry Harris on the desperate slide from Top Division pre-eminence to the grey despair of the old Third Division.

I loved every minute of the game.

My support is nothing compared to the dedicated few, who, for years, have given their time and passion to the club.

You should see them, in the supporters' club – talk about shock and awe. Only Basher Benfield forecast a season to remember, and his optimism was greeted with much shaking of heads. Well, Pompey fans are a pessimistic lot.

I sat down with a pint of Tetleys and bag of chips to discuss the happiest season for 50 years with three of the committee; Paddy Thomas, a retired teacher, businessman Mike Newman, the supporters' club's new chairman, and Andy Dobbs, who edits *True Blue*, the fanzine.

We all agreed that the side that beat Nottingham Forest in the first game of the season on a sunny Saturday August 10 was a revelation – maybe a sign of triumphs to come.

Paddy had seen signs of the revolution during the pre-season friendly with Celtic.

"Before that game, Harry Redknapp had been using all sorts of combinations, but, in the second half, he put out the team that played the way he wanted.

"Andy, with true Pompey scepticism, thought that, because they had won with such ease, it must have been because Forest were so awful."

Mike: "Harry Redknapp has turned out to be so much better a manager than I thought he would be. When Jim Smith came along, I really couldn't believe it."

Andy: "It was the best signing he made all season."

Mike: "It has given us such strength in depth. They must be the most respected managers in the First Division. We all thought he was wrong to sell Peter Crouch last season, but now he looks like a £5-million cart horse. No one rated Todorov as his replacement, but now it would be unthinkable without him. He epitomises the kind of team Harry has put together. You only have to compare him with Lee Bradbury (stalwart striker for many years). He has the same never-say-die attitude but Toddy has been quite outstanding. Truth is, Bradders is better suited to a side fighting relegation, which, of course, has always been his lot."

They are impressed with the way the club is managed at board level.

Mike: "I find I can pick up the phone and get straight through to Peter Storrie (the chief executive). It's a bit disconcerting finding someone in that position who is so friendly."

Paddy: "He gives a straight 'yes' or 'no' answer or promises to call back. He always does."

They recount with relish the night Jim Smith was due to attend one of the supporters' open evenings. Smith went to the wrong building, couldn't work out where he should be, and went home.

An anguished call to Peter Storrie had him downing a glass of barely-sipped wine and making an impromptu substitute's appearance.

But conundrums remain: will the club survive in the top league, will it have a stadium worthy of that status (as it is, Fratton Park is the sixth-smallest ground in the First Division), and will chairman Milan Mandaric be there with his wallet at the ready?

Andy: "The aim has to be finish in the third quarter, roundabout 16th."

Paddy: "I think we'll do it; we have the nucleus of a good side. Merson will still be fine, even though sometimes he has been flattered by playing some second-rate sides. Maybe he will benefit from not being marked man to man, the way he has been."

Andy: "I worry about the defence. Has De Zeeuw got the pace to handle Michael Owen or Thierry Henry? I doubt it."

Paddy: "I think we need at least four players and two of them should be full backs."

Andy: "We are a passing side, so much better than Leicester and much better than we were in 1987 (Portsmouth's last promotion year), when we ground out every result and always seemed to win 1-0."

Paddy: "We used to be so pessimistic, but this team is so confident and so good to watch. Just think of the number of times we have gone a goal down and still won."

Mike: "Sometimes I've found myself wishing we would go behind, just to make it more interesting."

Andy: "We can't be a team like West Brom, which relies so heavily on the passion of the fans. We have only got 19,000 of them. Survival depends on whether Milan is prepared to put his hand in his pocket. Don't forget that the last time we were in the Top Division, John Deacon, the chairman, took his hand out, sold key players, and we went straight back down."

They are unanimous that, if the club is to prosper, it has to progress steadily.

Mike – clearly careless of his future in the chairman's chair – actually praised S**th*mpt*n.

"I hate to say it, but they have handled their affairs very well. They have built the stadium and found another 15,000 fans. I know people knock the JCLs (Johnny Come Latelies) who have turned up this season, but we need them if we are going to have crowds as big as Southampton."

Andy: "Trouble is, we have been threatened with an announcement about the new stadium every other week. We are promised yet another in two weeks' time."

Paddy: "It is a big investment, but, once made, it makes Portsmouth a very attractive going concern with fantastic support."

They all perceive Mandaric – who clearly glories in the applause of the fans – as the key to survival.

Mike: "My fear is that now that we are up, Milan won't stay."

Paddy: "I worry that he might do an Al Fayed and leave the club in the same shambles as Fulham."

Mike: "I can't fathom what motivates him. He has 47,000 people working for him, he can live anywhere in the world, he can have all the helicopters and boats he fancies. It makes me wary. What's in it for him?"

Paddy: "It would be a very strange person who did not react to 19,000 fans singing your praises every week."

Andy: "It's no coincidence that, when he threatens to go, the chants are noisier than ever."

But none noisier than the one that rolled around the ground last Sunday: "To the Nationwide, bye, bye."

ANORAK'S CORNER

May 4
Bradford City 0 Portsmouth 5
Scorers: Festa (20), Todorov (48, 50, 58), Stone (67)
Crowd: 19,088
Team: Hislop (Kawaguchi), Foxe (O'Neil), Primus, De Zeeuw, Festa (Diabate), Quashie, Stone, Sherwood, Todorov, Aiyegbeni, Merson.
Substitutes: Pericard, Burton.

It was party day. 7,000 fans made the long journey to keep the celebrations bubbling, the team wore white boots supplied by Gianluca Festa's company, and Yoshi Kawaguchi came off the sub's bench for the first time all season. Oh, and Portsmouth won 5-0. Festa, who was playing his last game for the club, scored first, thanks to a hefty deflection off a defender. Todorov then hit a stunning hat trick in 10 minutes, bringing his total to 26. Stone scored the goal of the afternoon after he latched on to a breathtaking sequence of passes involving Merson and Todorov.

There will be more, many more entries for 'Arry's Bargain Basement over the summer. He has been quoted as saying he needs up to eight new players. Gianluca Festa, the cool-as-a-cucumber defender, has returned to Italy, Markus Heikkinen, who appeared for about thirty seconds, is on his way, and Jason Crowe and Sasha Ilic are sweating on new contracts. Redknapp has already been linked with an offer for Arsenal's Martin Keown (a sprightly 37 in July) and Kanu, as Arsene Wenger plans his own bargain hunt. Efstathios Tavlaridis, who played very solidly for Pompey when on loan, is also expected to leave Arsenal. Aiyegbeni Yakubu has signed, possibly for a club record of £2million, with both clubs sharing the proceeds if he is transferred, but the fate of Vincent Pericard – as big a favourite with the crowd as the electrifying Yakubu – is uncertain.

At last, at last, the announcement that has been promised since Milan Mandaric arrived: there will be a new stadium. A new 28,000 stadium is planned to be built within 20 months at a cost of £26million. Happily, it is thought – certainly hoped – that the mock-Tudor facade in Frogmore Road will be preserved, and, more importantly, once the development is finished, it will be bigger than the one our neighbours have just built down the road...

Nationwide Division 1
2002-2003 FINAL TABLE

Pos	Team	P	HOME					AWAY					GD	PTS
			W	D	L	F	A	W	D	L	F	A		
1	Portsmouth	46	17	3	3	52	22	12	8	3	45	23	52	98
2	Leicester	46	16	5	2	40	12	10	9	4	33	28	33	92
3	Sheff Utd	46	13	7	3	38	23	10	4	9	34	29	20	80
4	Reading	46	13	3	7	33	21	12	1	10	28	25	15	79
5	Wolves	46	9	10	4	40	19	11	6	6	41	25	37	76
6	Nottm For	46	14	7	2	57	23	6	7	10	25	27	32	74
7	Ipswich	46	10	5	8	49	39	9	8	6	31	25	16	70
8	Norwich	46	14	4	5	36	17	5	8	10	24	32	11	69
9	Millwall	46	11	6	6	34	32	8	3	12	25	37	-10	66
10	Wimbledon	46	12	5	6	39	28	6	6	11	37	45	3	65
11	Gillingham	46	10	6	7	33	31	6	8	9	23	34	-9	62
12	Preston	46	11	7	5	44	29	5	6	12	24	41	-2	61
13	Watford	46	11	5	7	33	26	6	4	13	21	44	-16	60
14	Crystal Pal	46	8	10	5	29	17	6	7	10	30	35	7	59
15	Rotherham	46	8	9	6	27	25	7	5	11	35	37	0	59
16	Burnley	46	10	4	9	35	44	5	6	12	30	45	-24	55
17	Walsall	46	10	3	10	34	34	5	6	12	23	35	-12	54
18	Derby	46	9	5	9	33	32	6	2	15	22	42	-19	52
19	Bradford	46	7	8	8	27	35	7	2	14	24	38	-22	52
20	Coventry	46	6	6	11	23	31	6	8	9	23	31	-16	50
21	Stoke	46	9	6	8	25	25	3	8	12	20	44	-24	50
22	Sheff Wed	46	7	7	9	29	32	3	9	11	27	41	-17	46
23	Brighton	46	7	6	10	29	31	4	6	13	20	36	-18	45
24	Grimsby	46	5	6	12	26	39	4	6	13	22	46	-37	39

APPENDIX I

SING WHEN YOU'RE WINNING

Yet another success story. Stadium DJ Steve Pearson overcame the shaky sound system to bring a little music into our lives. His upbeat style won him the Upshot Cup for the stadium announcer of the year. One of his gimmicks was to give each player a signature tune to celebrate to when they scored. Here is his Pompey hit parade:

Shaka Hislop: *Boom Shakalak* by Apache Indian

Linvoy Primus: *Jump Around* by House of Pain

Matthew Taylor: *Eat My Goal* by Collapsed Lung

Arjan De Zeeuw: *One Step Beyond* by Madness

Hayden Foxe: *Down Under* by Men at Work

Gianluca Festa: *The Addams Family* theme tune

Nigel Quashie: *Whoomps There It Is* by The Tag Team

Gary O'Neil: *Bohemian Like You* by the The Dandy Warhols

Lassina Diabate: *Dilemma* by Nelly and Kelly Rowland

Tim Sherwood: *Hey Baby* by DJ Otzi

Paul Merson: *Rollin'* by Limp Bizkit

Svetoslav Todorov: *Insane In The Membrane* by Cypress Hill

Deon Burton: *Who Let The Dogs Out?* by The Baha Men

Vincent Pericard: *Nuflow* by Big Bruvvaz

Yakubu Aiyegbeni: *Tide Is High* by Atomic Kitten

Steve Stone: *Hot in Here* by Nelly
Kevin Harper: *This is How We Do It* by Montell Jordan
Mark Burchill: *That's The Way (I Like It)* by KC and The Sunshine Band
Yoshikatsu Kawaguchi: *Turning Japanese* by The Vapors
Jason Crowe: *Gold* by Spandau Ballet

APPENDIX II

WHAT GOES UP...

How will the First Division champions fare in the Premiership next season? **Daniel Finkelstein,** of *The Times,* investigates:

When the apple fell on Sir Isaac Newton's head, he learnt the first law of football – what goes up, must come down. This is true of all aspects of the game, except penalties taken by Chris Waddle. Of course, it is promotion to the Premiership that provides the best example of this law. One year a team soars to the top of the First Division, the next they are struggling to avoid relegation. Just as birth is the only disease that is 100 per cent fatal, so the triumph of promotion brings the certainty of humbling encounters and nervous moments.

For Portsmouth fans, this season has bought exhilarating and surprising success, as chronicled weekly for *The Times* by Richard Holledge, in his Life and Chimes column. But what sort of reward awaits them in the Premier League? Is the bruising encounter with Manchester United in the FA Cup a foretaste of many such dispiriting games?

Using figures assembled to calculate the results in FA Cup games, Dr Alex Morton and Henry Stott have ranked the top 35 club sides based on their defensive and attacking strength. This creates a 'league table' of all clubs, regardless of division. The ranking gives a rough idea of what Portsmouth's division-topping performance really means when compared with Barclaycard Premiership sides.

It looks like a hard season ahead, but not a hopeless one. The statisticians place the Fratton Park boys 16th, just ahead of Fulham and comfortably ahead (Mr Redknapp will be satisfied to learn) of West Ham United. The ranking does not, however, correspond exactly to the real league table. Performance in previous seasons helps to determine strength. Liverpool, for instance, are ranked ahead of Newcastle United. As an indication of how seriously to take Morton and Stott's classification, it is worth looking at what it had to say last year. Manchester City's first division performance in 2001-02 placed them 8th in the overall ranking, and they duly thrived.

Portsmouth fans will probably not be surprised to learn of the hard fight ahead. For Sunderland, however, the work of Morton and Stott will come as a nasty shock. Their team are 35th, suggesting that a battle to avoid relegation to the Second Division looms, unless big changes are made. Wigan Athletic and Crewe Alexandra are comfortably ahead of the Premiership's bottom side.